**NO**NONSENSE

# THE
# MONEY CRISIS

How bankers grabbed
our money – and how
we can get it back

D1103564

## About the author

Peter Stalker is a writer and editor based in Oxford in the United Kingdom. His most recent books are the *No-Nonsense Guide to International Migration* (New Internationalist, 2008), the *Oxford Guide to Countries of the World* (Oxford University Press, 2007) and the *First Parliament of Asia: A history of the UN Economic and Social Commission for Asia and the Pacific* (Bangkok, ESCAP 2007).

He is a former co-editor of **New Internationalist** magazine and the editor of the initial series of *Human Development Reports* produced in the 1990s in New York by the United Nations Development Programme. He has a special interest in international migration on which he has worked as a consultant to the International Labour Organization, written three books, and maintains the online *Stalker's Guide to International Migration*. This and other sites are available from his website pstalker.com.

Although his early experience in development issues was in Latin America, most of his work in developing countries in recent years has been in Asia. In Bangkok, for example, he has worked with the United Nations in assessing the achievement of the Millennium Development Goals across Asia and the Pacific, and in Jakarta he has written a series of national human development reports for Indonesia. He has also worked on numerous reports on economic and social development for other international organizations.

**NO**NONSENSE

# THE
# MONEY CRISIS

## How bankers grabbed
## our money – and how
## we can get it back

PETER STALKER

**NewInternationalist**

# **NO**NONSENSE

**The Money Crisis:**
How bankers grabbed our money – and how we can get it back

Published in 2015 by
New Internationalist Publications Ltd
The Old Music Hall
106-108 Cowley Road
Oxford OX4 1JE, UK
**newint.org**

Adapted from No-Nonsense Guide to Global Finance (2009).

Cover design: Andrew Smith, asmithcompany.co.uk

Series editor: Chris Brazier
Series design by Juha Sorsa

Printed and bound in Great Britain by Bell & Bain Ltd, Glasgow
who hold environmental accreditation ISO 14001.

British Library Cataloguing-in-Publication Data.
A catalogue record for this book is available from the British Library.

Library of Congress Cataloging-in-Publication Data.
A catalog for this book is available from the Library of Congress.

ISBN 978-1-78026-241-3
(ISBN ebook 978-1-78026-242-0)

# Contents

# Foreword

For years, the world of finance had become more and more distant from the ordinary citizen, its dynamics increasingly shrouded by arcane terms such as short-selling, credit default swaps and securitization. With banks pushing credit cards on people, with seeming disregard for their credit history, and offering them mortgages at low interest rates, many were happy to be swept along by the financial flow without really understanding what was going on. When people were advised by bankers that keeping their money in savings accounts was old-fashioned, and they were foregoing tremendous profits by not putting their money in high-interest-bearing accounts that would allow the banks to make money for them, they were all too happy to oblige, accepting their banker's word that there was no way for them to lose.

In 2008 that fantastic world collapsed, and millions of unsuspecting citizens were dragged to the brink of personal disaster by forces they could not understand. The banks were bailed out with vast sums of taxpayers' money and the price of the resultant debts has been paid by ordinary people all over the world. Meanwhile the bankers and speculators have not only gone unpunished but have continued to rake in their huge bonuses.

Had Peter Stalker's concise explanation of the money crisis been available earlier, many people it might have reached may well have been more circumspect in relating to the financial economy. Stalker does an excellent job of deconstructing finance, taking us from the origins of money to the development of banks, on to the world of high finance, and on to the great crash of 2007-2008. Complex terms such as futures and derivatives are explained simply, though there is a limit to understanding the dynamics of some these instruments. Even the US billionaire investor Warren Buffet admitted he could not understand how derivatives worked, eventually calling them 'financial weapons of mass destruction'.

The author ends this NoNonsense book with many reasonable proposals to regulate finance. This writer would add others. I would abolish the G-20, the Financial Stability Forum, the Basel Process, and the IMF, and support the establishment of a global financial authority under the umbrella of the United Nations. The aim of financial reform must no longer be to allow a few to corner financial profits. It must be, as the author says, to get banking and finance back to its primordial task of connecting savers to the people who need the money.

**Walden Bello**
waldenbello.org
Author of *Capitalism's Last Stand* (Verso, 2013);
Adjunct Professor, State University of New York
at Binghamton; Member of the Board, Focus on the
Global South.

# Introduction

Sellers of *Situation Sthlm*, Sweden's street newspaper sold by the homeless, have now been given credit-card readers so that they can accept electronic payments instead of cash. Another step forward in what is already the world's most cashless society. The purchasers no longer have to contribute spare change, but what exactly are they offering? A few borrowed seconds of plastic, a sudden burst of digits across the ether, critical information about their whereabouts and their lifestyle choices, a new entry in a database, another line in a bank account? The answer is all of these things and more – all of which could be summed up as 'money'.

What exactly is money? Truth be told, there is no definitive answer. Clearly it is much more than coins in your purse or notes in your wallet, or even gold bars in a bank vault. But after that things get much fuzzier. Money is what money does. Ultimately, it is a system for measuring social relationships – helping define mutual rights and obligations. The cash and coins that we exchange are just tokens of that trust. Seen in this way, money and the monetary system that we use ought to be an essential element of the 'public realm'.

This principle of money as a 'public good' is reflected in the symbols of our currencies, reassuringly embossed as they are with the heads of monarchs and presidents and ornate national symbols. But what about a payment for *Situation Sthlm?* No sign of King Gustaf VI Adolf or any other Swedish notable. Instead you will probably have to make do with the logos of Visa or Mastercard, or maybe your bank. At this point money glides into the private realm. Not only is the payment a personal transfer, it has gone into a commercial money system.

This has long been the case. Money has evolved

differently in many societies, but has always involved complex interlocking roles and responsibilities combining public and private action. Nowadays we might assume that governments print or stamp out the money and that the banks then manage this, principally by taking savings and passing these on as loans. This is far from the case. In fact, most of the money circulating in our economies has been created by banks out of thin air.

We went along with this system while it appeared to work. We trusted our governments to control the money supply and regulate the banks. We trusted the banks to act legally and responsibly. Our faith was shattered by the 2008 global financial crisis. Governments and central banks struggled to manage flows of money, and greedy and incompetent financiers triggered a global economic crisis – plunging millions of innocent families into the misery of public austerity programs. Not everyone suffered. By and large the money men survived and prospered. Indeed they brazenly paid themselves even larger bonuses.

We cannot even rely on bankers for basic honesty. Banks around the world have been caught in a series of scandals ranging from abuse of power to malpractice to fraud. Between 2009 and 2013, a group of international banks were fined a total of $267 billion. This included rigging foreign-exchange markets, lying about interbank lending rates and mis-selling insurance.

These and many other banks were also implicated in the global financial crisis. In fact, however, this was as much a money crisis – which exposed fundamental flaws in our monetary systems. Worse, in trying to revive national economies by encouraging banks to lend more, we are now piling up more of the private debt that led to the crisis in the first place.

Instead we should pay more attention to money itself. Generally we take it for granted. We might worry about not having enough, but we do not worry about what money is or what it does. We need to pay closer attention because there is more going on than meets the eye. For example, when readers buy *Situation Sthlm* with a credit card they are not using existing Swedish kronor. Instead they will be transmitting new kronor generated by the credit-card company's computer. Buyer and seller might be satisfied with the transaction, but they have also unwittingly boosted the number of kronor in circulation, and thus the Swedish money supply.

The purpose of this book is to show why this matters, and why money should be created and controlled only by governments.

# 1 What is money?

**Money has flowed through human civilization for millennia, lubricating trade and other forms of exchange and taking on many forms – from wooden tally sticks to evanescent bits and bytes whizzing through the electronic ether. And as it moves from person to person, money talks – offering a running commentary on the balance of power between individuals, corporations and the state.**

FOR SOMETHING THAT plays such a central part in everyday life, money is remarkably slippery and amorphous. Is it an object, or just a piece of information? You can consider as money the coins in your pocket or the notes in your wallet. But if your total worldly wealth is on your person right now you are unlikely to feel very secure. You hope that the cash you have in your bank account also counts as money, though it may never have taken a physical form – just an electronic entry in some remote computer. Even some of the world's poorest communities are now receiving payments and settling accounts using mobile phones.

Money is what money does. Suppose you are in a taxi, discover that you have no cash and offer to pay with your watch. Is your watch money? If so, then absolutely anything could be money – which would make this a very fat book. Since the book is mercifully slim, there must be an escape route, via a snappy definition. One of the standard assertions is: 'Money is anything that is widely used for making payments and accounting for debts and credits.' Or, in more specific terms, money is anything that governments will accept for paying taxes.

## Credit and barter

Money has often been thought of as just like any other

commodity – part of a sophisticated form of barter. In fact money has its origins in credit as people tried to keep track of mutual obligations.[1] One the earliest types of record was the 'tally stick'. This would be a stick generally of hazel-wood on which details of the obligation were recorded, with notches and in writing. The stick was then split. The debtor kept one half; the creditor kept the other. Since each stick was unique the record would be quite specific. Its value depended, however, not on the price of hazel-wood but on the relationship between debtor and creditor.[2]

In principle the creditor could pass on the tally stick to someone else and indeed this often happened. This would make the tally stick a limited form of money. However, another option might be to use something else as an intermediate token or commodity – a more general 'medium of exchange'. For this purpose you could use any readily transferable item but the best bet will be something in limited supply. Throughout the ages the most common tokens have been made of precious metals, and particularly silver and gold, which have the merit of being relatively scarce and portable while also being divisible into any size and weight.

Metals are durable, which is why even when many other elements of ancient cultures have disappeared, pieces of metallic money often remain as the most persistent vestiges of human activity. This might suggest that most transactions were carried out with cash, but many more took the form of credit, even if any records of transactions have long since vanished.

The earliest known usages of commodities as money tokens have been traced back to the 24th century BCE, in Mesopotamia, the land between the Tigris and Euphrates rivers, which is now shared between Iraq, Syria and Turkey. Here people often used both silver and grain when exchanging goods. They could also use these for paying fines. Around 1000 BCE the king of Eshnunna in northern

Mesopotamia, for example, declared that the fine for biting a man's nose was around half a kilo of silver.[3]

Of course metals that are scarce in some places can be quite common in others. So if you lived in, or better yet owned, a place that had a gratifying supply of precious metals, you would literally be sitting on a goldmine. Lydia, for example, a territory in what is now Turkey, was well endowed with a natural gold-silver alloy called electrum. The last king of Lydia, from 560 BCE, was Croesus, who became fabulously wealthy; indeed he was 'as rich as Croesus'.

## Slotting in coins

Lydia is also thought to have been the first place to introduce coins – casting different weights of gold or silver so as to offer a system of regular oval pieces stamped on either face with different symbols according to the value. Instead of carrying around a pair of scales to tell how much metal you were exchanging you could instead accept the coins at 'face value'.

Coins were also being produced in city states in ancient Greece. In Athens, for example, the government would pay citizens with coins for public-service activities, from fighting (as soldiers) to taking turns in juries. At first the face value of the coins supposedly matched the value of the metal they contained. But this would prove awkward for the smallest transactions which might require tiny scraps of silver, so the Greek cities also started to issue bronze coins, simply asserting their value, which was generally greater than their metal content. This represented an early example of what might be called 'fiat' money.[4] Indeed, even the gold and silver coins were often irregular so they too relied on the fiat element. In fact, the use of gold and silver in some respects confuses the issue, implying that money is a commodity like any other when it is more a token that represents a recognized debt.

Soon Athens was making similar declarations about gold or silver coins, imposing a value higher than the actual metal content. It could do this by ensuring that only the state could produce the coins and making it clear that it would prosecute any forgers. This was also an early example of 'seigniorage' – the power over money creation that allows the government to manufacture money and use it to pay its own bills. Athens also saw the first signs of what we now call bankers. These started out as money changers, providing foreigners arriving in the city with coins they would need for daily trans-actions. But some money-changers also started to store coins, and to lend them out – at an interest rate of around 12 per cent a year.

To make the value readily identifiable, the coins were originally stamped with symbols such as plants or animals. In Athens, for example, one of the coins carried a stamp of the city's sacred bird and became known as an 'owl'. Eventually, however, the temptation for rulers to portray themselves on the coinage proved irresistible. The first monarch of this era to decide that coins would look better if adorned with his face was Alexander the Great who, by around the third century BCE, had conquered most of the known world and felt entitled to lord it over its money as well.

## When in Rome

A couple of centuries later the Romans too took up the idea of making coins. They also introduced some of our modern terminology. One of the first places they used to manufacture coins was near a temple located on the Capitol, the citadel of Rome. The goddess occupying that temple was Juno Moneta, from whom are derived the words 'money' and the place where coins are made, the 'mint'. Juno's function as a goddess, appropriately enough for this risky item, was the 'one who warns'.

In Rome the basic unit of currency was the bronze

coin, the 'as', which was literally the value of an ass. The principal silver coin was named the denarius, which in 212 BCE could buy 10 asses. The Romans also gave an early indication of the power of money, or at least the power of money backed by brute force. As they crushed other regimes across Europe they grabbed most of the local precious metals. In 167 BCE, when the Romans defeated the kingdom of Macedon, for example, they marched off with a cool 324,000 kilograms of silver, equivalent to 75 million denarii. In this way they cornered most of the available silver and ensured that the denarius would become the major currency in the western Mediterranean.

In Europe nowadays, if you dig up ancient coins, the chances are they will be Roman. This is because, in the second and third century BCE, the Romans minted many millions of them. However, since even they could not seize sufficient precious metal to make these coins, they steadily reduced the silver content. In the mid-260s CE in Britain, which the Romans had conquered, they replaced the denarius with the 'radiate', which by then was down to just 0.5 per cent silver. This did not prove very popular. Britons and others started to turn their noses up at coins whose value was set by imperial decree and reverted to weighing out precious metal. Indeed, following the collapse of the Roman Empire, most of the barbarian kingdoms wisely stuck to gold.

The seventh century saw the emergence of the first Muslim communities – spreading out from Mecca, one of the principal trading cities of Arabia, to establish a caliphate that would eventually extend from what is now Afghanistan right across to Spain. They too started to use coins. The prophet Muhammad himself was generally uneasy about money and is supposed to have said 'money puts my community to the test'. But his victorious followers found it easier to go with the financial flow, and generally absorbed the monetary systems of the countries they conquered, though carefully replacing any Christian crosses with Islamic symbols that varied according to the religious orientation of the ruler, Sunni or Shi'a. Initially they used gold, largely from Africa, but later switched to silver. By the 11th century in Egypt, one dinar, derived from the Latin 'denarius aureus', could pay for a servant for a month, or buy around 100 kilograms of wheat.

## China's 'little brothers'

Coins were also appearing on the other side of the world. In China at around the same time, when the kings were trading they sometimes used various commodities, including grain or cloth or knives or spades. But gradually they too started to adopt forms of token payment through coins. At first they felt more comfortable if these actually looked like miniature spades or knives. But eventually they found it easier to make metal disks. Distinctively, they punched a square hole in the middle, to make the coins easier to carry in bulk by passing a string through the hole. The Chinese are also fervent believers in the power of luck and some of their coins, particularly during the 10th century, were considered very auspicious and were known as 'little brothers'. Across Asia you can still buy these, and their multiple successors and copies, as amulets or temple souvenirs.

Unlike European rulers, the Chinese royals and nobles resisted the temptation to put their own faces on the coins. Indeed it would not be until 1912 that the first Chinese face appeared – that of Sun Yat-sen, president of the newly formed Republic of China. China also originated paper money. But it seemed in no hurry to do so. Having invented paper around 100 CE the Chinese did not produce their first paper money until 1,000 years or so later, during the Song dynasty. This was a matter of convenience. At that point, China was divided up into many regions, each of which used its own currency, often in the form of low-value iron coins. Moreover, some regions forbade the export of coins. Itinerant merchants found this very awkward, and so started to buy goods not with coins, but with 'exchange notes', a kind of IOU which promised to pay the bearer the appropriate amount of cash or gold at a later date in a more convenient place. If the buying merchant who wrote the note had a good reputation, then that note, before it expired, was as good as gold.

Later, Chinese rulers latched on to this innovation and started to issue such notes themselves. But they did not put any time limit, and offered the more general promise to the bearers that they could exchange the notes at the mint for gold or silver or, if preferred, less-tattered notes. By the time of the Mongol Yuan dynasty, from the 13th century, the government permitted only paper money. When the Venetian merchant Marco Polo arrived in 1275, he discovered that China, as so often, was some way ahead of the rest of the world.

## Pounds to pesos to dollars

London, by contrast, in the first millennium CE was still in the numismatic dark ages. Indeed, even coinage was rare until the eighth century when King Offa of Mercia issued the first silver penny. Subsequently some of the Saxon kingdoms started to issue silver coins, known as 'sterlings', of which they could turn out around 240 from a pound weight of silver. Hence the term a pound of sterlings, later abbreviated to a 'pound sterling'. At this point most documents were written in Latin, in which the word for pound is 'libra', which is why the symbol for the pound is a crossed L, or £ in its more ornate form. Eventually, after the Normans conquered England, they developed an accounting system that also involved 240 pennies to the pound. This was to last, though with pennies made of copper, until 1971 when the UK decimalized the coinage, retaining the pound but dividing it instead into 100 pence – popularly, if inelegantly, abbreviated to 'pee'.

Elsewhere in Europe there were the first stirrings of the almighty dollar. One origin was the St Joachim valley in what is now the Czech Republic, which had a number of silver mines. The German for valley is *Tal* and the coins produced there were often called thalers. This suffered many variations in spelling and pronunciation and, given the well-known gift for languages among English-speaking peoples, the thaler was often mispronounced as the dollar.

Other coins in continental Europe at this time included in Spain the 'peso' which is simply Spanish for 'weight'. The prosaic peso does, however, have the distinction of having provoked an early example of global inflation. In 1544 the *conquistadores* who were trampling across South America came across in Potosí, in what is now Bolivia, a mountain which consisted largely of silver ore. For three or more centuries they excavated this treasure trove, delivering in all more than 62,000 metric tons of silver to Spain. This was an excellent result for the Spanish, who used this to pay off many of their debts. But it was less beneficial for the toiling Amerindian miners who dug out the ore, largely as slave labor. And it was also a mixed blessing for many other people back in continental Europe since, over the period 1500 to 1600 as the silver flowed across the Atlantic, prices rose fivefold. This was then transmitted to other countries. In England, for example, in the 200 years or so following the discovery of the Americas, prices rose three and a half times.[5] If the citizens of Europe had not heard about the discovery of the New World in any other way, they would have felt the impact in their pockets.

The peso was also widely used in Britain's American colonies. Here it became known as the Spanish milled thaler or dollar. So when the US designated its own currency in 1792 it also adopted the word dollar. But where did the $ sign come from? Surprisingly, its origins have been lost. One explanation is that it came from the standard abbreviation of the peso, a P, for which the plural was PS. If you just keep the vertical stroke of the P and superimpose the S on it you get the $. Quite so. On the other hand, the dollar sign often has two vertical strokes, prompting another explanation. The Spanish dollar had two vertical lines on the reverse to represent the Pillars of Hercules, and it is said that these lines eventually got transferred to the US dollar. Since no-one is entirely sure where the $ came from, feel free to invent your own explanation.

## Finding funny money

Of course not everyone was trading with coins. A favorite observation of Europeans travelling to exotic parts was that these foreigners seemed to be using many odd things for money. Travellers venturing across Africa and the Pacific, for example, often 'discovered' people exchanging a wide variety of objects. One of the most common was salt. In 1520 a Portuguese visitor to what is now Ethiopia found people trading with blocks of salt 'cut out of mountains'. English colonists in North America found the native people in Virginia using clam shells, while visitors to parts of India found local people using cowrie shells. Travellers to the Pacific encountered an even more diverse array of possibilities including teeth and, in one of the more arcane options, 'the little feathers near the eye of fowls'.[6]

While these make for curious travellers' tales they probably say more about the perceptions of the colonists than about the places they visited. For one thing, many of these countries had previously used coins: the kings of Ethiopia, for example, following Roman influences, had issued coins from the third to the seventh centuries. And India, following Greek patterns, had a long and sophisticated tradition of coinage from the fourth century, which by the 16th century had flowered into more than 300 types of *rupya* (Hindi for 'silver coin').

The predilection for spotting curious types of money resulted partly from the limitations of the new arrivals who, puzzled by complex cultures they could not understand, tended to reduce them to their own simple terms. In fact many of the exchanges they observed were concerned not with commerce but with religion or social customs or hierarchy. These might indeed involve a ritual exchange of cloth or shells but not as a commercial transaction.

One example is the Lele people in what is now the Democratic Republic of Congo who exchanged cloth woven from raffia. For centuries the Lele, under Belgian colonial rule, were all too familiar with the experience of laboring for Belgian francs. But they also had a wide variety of other circumstances in which, for the purposes of forging social ties, the only acceptable payment was cloth – for fees to traditional healers, for example, or fines for adultery, or as gifts to mark rites of passage.

In fact money is often strange, but not because of peculiar forms of currency. All over the world money has evolved and mutated. Nowadays it is a complex phenomenon, based on indirect forms of credit, and appearing and disappearing at the stroke of a pen – largely because of the invention of banking, which is the focus of the next chapter.

**1** F Martin, *Money, the unauthorized biography,* The Bodley Head, London, 2013. **2** A Mitchell Innes, 'What is Money?' in *Credit and State Theories of Money – The Contributions of A Mitchell Innes*, Edward Elgar, Cheltenham, 2004. **3** C Eagleton and J Williams, *Money: A history,* British Museum Press, London, 2007. **4** J Cribb, *Money: From Cowrie Shells to credit cards*, British Museum Publications, London, 1986. **5** JK Galbraith, *Money: Whence It came, Where It Went*, Houghton Mifflin Company, Boston, 1975. **6** Eagleton and Williams, op cit.

# 2 The creation of banks

People with money or other valuables looked for ways of keeping these safe, by storing them in the vaults of goldsmiths or pawnbrokers. But then something strange happened. These canny operatives started to multiply the contents of their vaults. And nowadays their heirs, the commercial banks, similarly create money out of thin air, or out of flows of electrons. Governments have tried to manage this financial fecundity through their central banks but have never fully succeeded.

Having pondered on the origins of cash and coinage, it is now time to take a closer look at banks. Banking too has an ancient history regularly punctuated with sorry tales of greed and disaster. The money-changers in Rome were some of the earliest practitioners. Mostly, however, they did not lend money but just changed some of the gold or silver coins of foreign traders into the denarii that could be used when operating in Rome. Indeed the word 'bank' derives from the benches, called 'bancu', from which these and other proto-bankers plied their trade. You will not be surprised that they soon also needed a term for a bank failure – 'bankrupt' – which corresponds to someone taking a sledgehammer to the aforementioned bench to signal the demise of the enterprise.

Banks lend money, charging varying prices for their services through rates of 'interest'. This word derives from medieval Latin, from 'inter' meaning 'between', and 'esse' to 'be'. The lender was said to 'have an interest' in the transactions for which their money had been borrowed, and interest subsequently came to refer to the level of compensation they charged for being deprived of the funds while someone else used them.

The more devoutly religious considered this process abhorrent since it involved monetizing time – over which only the deity should have domain. They thus considered charging interest as an attempt to usurp divine power and condemned it as the sin of usury. It should be noted, however, that interest does not just involve considerations of time, but also takes into account the risk that the borrower might never repay.

Christians became more relaxed about the concept of interest from around the 11th century, not least because they wanted to borrow funds to finance wars against other religious groups – Muslims primarily, but also Jews or Orthodox Christians, or indeed anyone who rejected the authority of the Pope. This involved a series of crusades, the first of which aimed to retake Jerusalem from its Islamic occupants. From the 13th to the 15th centuries, these punitive expeditions were financed by wealthy enterprises in Venice and Genoa.

Pious though they may have been, these financiers required compensation, so they carefully devised ways of charging that made lending seem less sinful. Eventually the word usury became confined to lending at rates of interest that are excessive, though what constitutes excess is always a matter of judgment. Payday lenders are notorious for charging stratospheric rates of interest of 2,000 per cent or more – usury by any standard – but even people borrowing from Visa or MasterCard will face annual interest rates of 25 per cent or more. To this day, Islam forbids charging any interest, though Islamic scholars will advise financiers on how to get round this constraint, for a fee.

## The making of modern banking

By the 17th century, elements of modern banking were starting to emerge. At that time one of the main centers of international trade was Amsterdam. The busy merchants of the city, who had money pouring in from all directions, soon found themselves dealing with a baffling array of coinage. The Dutch Republic alone had at least 14 mints that were turning out coins of all different sizes, shapes and qualities – which were then mingled with all the cash arriving from overseas. In 1606 the Dutch parliament issued a guide for the perplexed – a money-changer's manual which listed no fewer than 341 silver and 505 gold coins.

This period amply demonstrated that 'bad money drives out good' – a principle articulated in 1558 by the financial agent of Queen Elizabeth I of England, Thomas Gresham, and known thereafter as Gresham's Law. If, for example, you have what you consider an iffy dollar bill, you will be tempted to palm it off on someone else as soon as possible, while keeping in your wallet all the other bills you believe to be the genuine article. In the 16th century people had much the same attitude to coins, especially those which looked as though they might have had some of their gold clipped off. The clipped coins naturally circulated the fastest. One of the neatest anti-clipping measures was devised by the ever-busy Sir Isaac Newton who, in addition to explaining the laws of motion, and devising the infinitesimal calculus and so much more, also became warden of the Royal Mint in 1696 and suggested milling fine lines into the edges of coins so as to make any clipping more obvious.[1]

## Dodgy coins

Coping with all this dubious coinage was at best inconvenient and at worst exposed the merchants and their customers to fraud. To cut through this financial clutter, in 1609 the City of Amsterdam established what we might now call a public bank. This cheerfully allowed people to deposit all their coins, but did so with due skepticism, evaluating their true worth by checking their weight and quality. After making a deduction for expenses, the bank would then note the true value of the coins and keep them in storage. The depositor could use these verified coins to make payments to another customer by asking the bank to shift them to that person's storage box. The owners of the coins thus had simple 'bank accounts'. This proved such a useful function that similar banks were established in other cities across Europe.

This also opened up opportunities for lending. If one Dutch merchant was short of cash, he or she could negotiate directly with another of the bank's customers for a loan at an agreed rate of interest. The lender could thus instruct the bank to move the coins to the borrower's storage box or, more likely, just to transfer ownership by changing a few numbers in their ledgers. Once the transfer had taken place, the lender started to earn interest, but also had to accept the risk that the borrower might default. The banks soon realized, however, that with so much unused cash in their vaults they too could use it to make loans, with or without the explicit consent of the depositors.

Something similar was happening with goldsmiths and pawnbrokers. In London in the 17th century, faced with multiple risks of plague, fire and war, many people would leave their gold coins and other valuables with various businesses for safekeeping – in particular those with strong vaults. To this day the official arbiter of British coinage is the Goldsmiths' Company of the City of London.[2] To recognize that they held these valuables, the goldsmiths would issue receipts or 'notes'. If the depositor later wished to 'spend' their valuables for some purpose they could present the note and ask for them back. However, they might find it more convenient just to spend the notes. If the goldsmith was reputable, the receipt itself was 'as good as gold' and anyone holding it could go to the goldsmith and take the metal itself. This is thought to be the origin of the 'promissory note' – what we would now think of as a banknote.

Then some enterprising goldsmith took an important new step by handing notes not just to depositors but also to people who wanted to borrow money and were prepared to pay interest. These notes did not correspond to any particular deposit of gold but rather reflected the fact that there was a lot of gold in the vaults. Nevertheless, the goldsmiths still required a reassuring amount of gold and needed to attract more deposits. They thus started offering interest to the depositors.

You will have noticed a sleight of hand which, if not actually dishonest, is at best risky. If everyone awkwardly shows up with their notes simultaneously demanding the equivalent in gold or coins they might be disappointed. Once depositors suspect their funds may not be available for withdrawal, they are apt to bang on the doors, asking for their money back – and thus triggering a 'run on the bank'. Regrettably, that was the ultimate fate of the Bank of Amsterdam. Having lent out too much to the Dutch East India Company and to the City of Amsterdam, it was forced to limit withdrawals and in 1819, after two decades of operation, had to be wound up.

Nevertheless, it had helped to establish a general model of banking that has survived largely intact. This is partly because it has proved useful for both borrowers and lenders. When Willie Sutton, a notorious bank robber in New York in the 1930s, was asked why he robbed banks, he famously replied: 'Because that's where the money is.'

To disguise the inherent risk, banks have done all they can to appear solid institutions. In the past, they tended to construct even their smallest branches to look as imposing as possible – sometimes with stout Greco-Roman porticos that looked as though they could withstand several earthquakes. And bank managers, until recently at least, also wore very sober suits, and were considered the epitome of respectability.

Even so, to this day, what banks do is essentially a conjuring trick. In fact they do not wait for anyone to make a deposit before making a loan. If they think that the borrower looks creditworthy they simply open a bank account and declare that the borrower has those funds in it. As the Canadian-born economist JK Galbraith memorably put it: 'The process by which banks create money is so simple that the mind is repelled. Where something so important is involved a deeper mystery seems only decent.'

Is the loan really money? Yes it is. The borrower can write a cheque, or make a bank transfer, on this amount to buy goods. If this transaction is with another customer of the same bank then the funds are transferred from one to the other. If the check is paid into an account in another bank much the same situation applies, except that there has to be an exchange between banks. In practice the major banks have a huge number of mutual transactions every day, most of which cancel out. But what if they do not? Enter the central bank.

## Central banks

Each country that issues its own currency has a central bank. In the US, for example, this is the Federal Reserve. In Australia it is the Reserve Bank of Australia. In Canada it is the Bank of Canada. There are also central banks for countries that share a currency; in the case of the euro, this is the European Central Bank. While you might assume that central banks are government operations, in fact many started out as private companies. The Reserve Bank of India, for example, was established in 1935 as a private company, though it was nationalized at independence in 1949.

The oldest of the central banks is the Bank of England which was founded in 1694 by a Scotsman, William Paterson. At that time the King of England, William III, also known as William of Orange, was in dire need of funds, not least because of his frequent quarrels with France. Paterson came up with a solution. He would create a new bank and sell shares in it. Then he could lend all the proceeds to the King, who could use these funds to fight the French. Paterson's proposal went down well. The King awarded the Bank of England a Royal Charter and promptly borrowed all the capital – £1.2 million. Previously all banks had been privately owned. Paterson's Bank of England, however, was to be a 'joint stock' company. This meant that it would not only raise its initial capital funds by selling shares but would also be a 'limited' company, so if it collapsed its owners would not have to pay debtors out of their own pockets – they had limited liability, in other words.

At the same time the Bank of England was a commercial operation that could take deposits and make loans. The fact that the King had already walked off with all the bank's subscribed funds, and thus its capital, was not a problem since he had left an IOU. The King was a decent credit risk and was likely to repay eventually, if only by taxing his citizens. This meant that the shareholders got double value for their investment. First, the King was paying interest on the loans. Second, based on his £1.2 million the bank could lend out the same amount in banknotes – it could 'monetize' the debt for other profitable lending through the issue of Bank of England banknotes. King William was much impressed by this wizardry and wanted further loans, requiring the Bank to raise yet more capital by selling more shares. The Bank of England had thus issued the notes that formed the British money supply based on a royal debt. To this day the British Crown has not repaid this. Indeed, it has been argued that, if it did, the entire British monetary system would collapse.[3]

The new Bank of England maintained a reputation for sound management. It ensured that it always kept enough coins on hand so that anyone who presented one of its notes was promptly repaid in silver or gold coins. But since the bank had government backing, few people actually tried to redeem their notes. At that point other English banks were also still issuing notes, but these were considered less reliable and thus less acceptable for payment. Soon most of the notes in circulation were those of the Bank of England. Nevertheless, it did occasionally run into problems after it issued large numbers of notes and at one point was forced temporarily to suspend the right of bearers to redeem their notes for gold or silver. To correct this tendency to overlend, in 1844 a new Bank Charter established that the Bank could only print additional notes that corresponded to the gold and silver that it maintained in its vaults – akin to what would later be called the 'gold standard'.

At that point, in most respects, the Bank of England remained just one commercial bank among many. In time, however, it started to take on what we now recognize to be the functions of a central bank. Not only did it have a quasi-monopoly on the right to issue paper money, it also became responsible for the control of other banks.

Nowadays, if any company wants to become a bank, they need a banking licence. This brings certain privileges but also a degree of regulation. The main privilege is that they can create deposits out of thin air and lend them to customers. Other institutions, such as savings and loan institutions, are allowed to make loans but these have to be with funds that have been saved with them. They are not allowed to create money. A banking licence thus sounds like a licence to print money, and in many respects it is.

But there are limitations. One is that every licensed bank is required to maintain a substantial sum at the central bank in the form of 'central bank reserves'. Another is a requirement for the bank to hold enough 'liquid assets' to meet potential withdrawals – which could be central bank reserves or government bonds or cash. Originally in the UK this was fixed as a set percentage or 'fraction' of all its outstanding loans. Should the percentage drop below this critical level, it would need topping up, by offering the central bank government bonds, for example, or by borrowing from the central bank at the prevailing interest rates. This system is known as 'fractional reserve banking'. The UK subsequently dropped this reserve ratio and instead now tries to achieve the same thing by requiring important banks to pass a 'stress test', to check that they can withstand a crisis. Other countries, including the US, still maintain such a ratio, also called a liquidity ratio, of around 10 per cent. Canada and Australia, like the UK, do not.

This also addresses the issue of how to resolve payments between banks. If one bank owes a net amount to another, this can ultimately be settled by making transfers between their reserve accounts at the central bank.

## Pulling the monetary levers

In countries such as India, where the state owns many of the banks that lend funds to the general public, it is easy enough for the government both to dictate to banks and to control the money supply. In most developed countries, however, the banks have largely been independent commercial enterprises so the central bank has to exert control indirectly. Although the terminology differs from country to country, the means are more or less common.

The first lever of control is through interest rates. Interest rates can be thought of as the charge for renting out money. If you were renting someone a car you would take into account many factors. What is the risk that the renter might drive off into the sunset and never return?

What could I otherwise have done with the car during that time? Will the engine wear out during that period? What are other people charging for that kind of car?

Renting out money involves similar considerations. You have to assess the risk that the borrower might default or disappear. You have to consider the rate of inflation, and thus the likelihood that when you get your money back it will be worth less. And of course you have to check what your competitor banks are offering since they might undercut your rates.

Within these constraints, banks can charge whatever they like. But they are also influenced by what the central bank declares to be the 'minimum lending rate' – in the US the 'discount rate'. This is the rate at which the central bank will lend to the commercial banks. They may, for example, need to borrow from the central bank if they have to boost their central bank reserves, or they need a reliable source of ready cash should they be faced with a sudden bout of withdrawals. The commercial banks can smooth out some of these daily fluctuations by borrowing from each other, but they also have the option of borrowing from the central bank. Commercial banks making loans to their customers will generally use the central bank rate as a starting point, while adding a percentage point or two to cover their expenses, the likelihood of default, and the desired profits.

## Interest rates

When it comes to setting interest rates, governments have several things to worry about. The first is inflation. The Bank of England, for example, is charged by the British government with the responsibility of keeping inflation below 2 per cent. If the Bank sees inflation creeping up, it may therefore decide to increase interest rates. Higher interest rates will discourage borrowing, or encourage people to repay existing loans, which can reduce the money supply and economic activity and thus help dampen inflation. If the central bank raises the rate at which it lends to commercial banks, this puts pressure on the banks to pass on the costs to their customers by raising the interest rates they themselves are charging.

The other main consideration when setting interest rates is employment. Stifling economic activity may have the merit of reducing inflation. This is fine if most working people have jobs. But there is always the risk of overdoing it, of slowing the economy down so much that there is a rise in unemployment. So governments have to strike a balance. Interest rates too low: inflation. Interest rates too high: unemployment.

This may give the impression that it is possible to fine-tune the economy to achieve the optimum balance. If only. In practice, economies respond to changes in interest rates, if at all, in the same way the proverbial oil tanker responds to a tweak to the tiller. The response time can be very long, up to a year; indeed, so long that, by the time any interest-rate changes take effect, the circumstances might have changed so dramatically that the central bankers would have been better steering in the opposite direction. And even if the general course was correct, there is always the risk of undershooting or overshooting. In the UK, the decisions are made by a group of wise persons, the Monetary Policy Committee, which generally changes rates quite slowly, typically by one quarter of one percentage point in either direction. Because these changes are so small, they are generally quoted in smaller units. One percentage point can also be referred to as 100 'basis points' – so in this case the change would be only 25 basis points.

This interest-rate tinkering appeared to work until the financial crisis. After this the situation became so dire that governments desperate to revive their ailing economies slashed interest rates so that they were close to zero – where they have remained ever since. This particular lever thus got stuck and could do little more to stimulate the economy. In fact, banks were reluctant to lend money at any interest rate because of fears that the borrowers would go bust.

## The Libor scandal

Banks are not forced to take loans from the central bank. They can instead borrow ready cash from elsewhere, including from each other in what is called the 'interbank' market. Ultimately, the rate at which they do so will be set by market forces – by the amount of spare cash the banks have at the time. The actual rate in London, for example, is called the London Interbank Offered Rate – Libor – which is also used as a reference point for banks elsewhere and for credit-card companies. Until recently, Libor was based on a fairly casual reporting system on the assumption that the bankers would simply tell the truth. This was a mistake. In 2008, it was revealed that for many years bankers had often chosen to lie, saying that they could borrow more cheaply than they actually could, so that they would appear to be in a healthier position than they really were – which is fraud. In 2013, the Royal Bank of Scotland, for example, acknowledged that, between 2006 and 2010, 21 traders and one manager had tried to rig Libor. To settle US and UK investigations, it agreed to pay fines of $612 million.[4]

Lending between banks, honest or not, might seem to cut the central bank out of the picture. But not entirely. The central bank itself also intervenes through what are called 'open-market operations'. If it wants to reduce the amount of cash in the banking system it has the option not only of increasing the base rate but also of hoovering up some cash by offering to sell government bonds at attractive rates. As will be explained later, a bond is a promise to pay whoever buys it a certain sum of money each year and to return the whole sum after a pre-determined period. Once these government bonds have been sold, they can then be traded on the open market. If, on the other hand, the central bank wants to stimulate economic activity because it is worried about rising unemployment and wants to increase the money supply, it does the reverse. It goes back to the bond market offering to pay whatever it takes to buy back such bonds, thus injecting more cash into the system.

On occasion, however, banks may be so chronically short of money, and nervous that fellow banks might go bust overnight, that they refuse to lend to them at any interest rate. This was the situation following the credit crunch from 2008. Banks hit by losses stemming, among other things, from mortgage defaults in the US, were so spooked that they clung onto the cash they had, so that interbank credit largely dried up. In these circumstances, the central bank can deploy another of its weapons, by acting as a 'lender of last resort'. If a commercial bank is basically solvent – in that it has sufficient deposits and capital, but just does not have enough funds readily available to pay immediate needs – the central bank can lend it funds and avoid an unnecessary collapse.

## Solvents and liquids

At this stage it is worth mulling over what 'solvent' means. If you have simple financial affairs and have $20,000 in the bank and total outstanding bills of only $10,000, then you are solvent. On the other hand, if you only have $10,000 but owe $20,000 you are in a less happy position. As an individual, you may not worry about this, on the grounds that you have a job which keeps enough money flowing in to pay the interest on the loans. But technically, if you have no other assets, you are insolvent. This is more of a problem for companies, including banks, which legally are not allowed to continue trading while insolvent. If you are insolvent, then creditors may take you to court to have you declared legally bankrupt.

But being insolvent is not the same as being 'illiquid'. You might think that being illiquid – which sounds equivalent to solid – is a good thing. But for a bank it can be a problem. Return to the situation where you were declared technically insolvent, but then you suddenly remembered that you owned a house worth $100,000. Immediately you realize that you are solvent. Phew! However, because most of your assets are tied up in bricks and mortar and you don't have much ready cash, you are considered illiquid. In the long term you should be OK but in the short term you may need to borrow some money to pay your immediate bills, perhaps using your house as security.

Banks too can be solvent but illiquid. They might, for example, lend someone the cash to buy a house and not expect to see all the money back for 20 years. This loan represents an asset for the bank but not one it can use immediately, so if it were faced with a lot of withdrawals it could face a liquidity crisis. While it is still probably solvent, since the loans it made still count as assets, it has nevertheless become illiquid.

## The lender of last resort

In this case it may well need to borrow from the central bank – the lender of last resort. The Bank of England took on this responsibility from around 1825. Recognizing the value of having a central bank for these and other purposes, many other countries followed suit. The Banque de France emerged from 1800 and in 1875 the Bank of Prussia became the Reichsbank. The US equivalent, the Federal Reserve System (the 'Fed'), was created in 1913 following a series of financial panics. The Fed is not just one institution but a system, which includes a central governmental agency in Washington DC, a Board of Governors, and 12 regional Federal Reserve Banks, which perform central banking functions within their own regions. The most important of these is the Federal Reserve Bank of New York which, as well as regulating New York banks, is responsible for the Fed's open-market operations.

Having a 'lender of last resort' offers a degree of security. The downside is 'moral hazard' – a situation where people protected from the consequences of their actions are tempted to take greater risks. Bankers, knowing that they have a central bank safety net, may make dangerous bets in search of higher profits and personal bonuses. Even if the bets fail, the bank is likely to survive. Governments will step in because bank failures are dangerous. Politicians fear the fallout from angry small depositors, but also know that the banks are intricately interconnected through webs of interbank lending so that the failure of one bank to repay an overnight loan could topple many other dominoes.

Another concern is that the central banks themselves might be subject to political manipulation. A government approaching an election may, for example, be tempted to reduce interest rates and expand the money supply to make people feel suddenly richer, even though soon after the election this could cause inflation. To guard against this 'boom and bust' strategy, most central banks in developed countries operate with a degree of independence. This can be achieved partly through long-term directorships. Although the directors or governors of central banks are political appointees, their terms of office will generally extend beyond the life of most governments. In the US, for example, the seven board members of the Fed are appointed for a term of 14 years, with one member's term expiring every other year. Nevertheless, the independence of central banks has limits. In practice most governments at times of economic crisis lean on central banks to take politically expedient decisions.

The Bank of England was nationalized in 1947 and essentially acted as a part of the government. But from

1997 it was granted operational independence, which meant that it was given the overall task of managing interest rates and the money supply. As noted earlier, it has been charged with keeping inflation at around two per cent – but is free to adjust interest rates as it sees fit in order to achieve this. The European Central Bank, which is in charge of monetary policy in those countries using the euro, has a similar target, as does the Bank of Canada. For the Reserve Bank of Australia the target is two to three per cent and for the Reserve Bank of New Zealand it is one to three per cent. In the US the Fed has two targets. The first is concerned with keeping down inflation, the other with maintaining high levels of employment. This is a trickier task since the two targets often conflict.

## Policing the banks

As well as managing interest rates and acting as lenders of last resort, some central banks may also be charged with policing their country's banks by monitoring their activities to ensure that they behave responsibly – and will not need bailing out. For this purpose they keep an eye on bank reserves and capital. They may want banks to have a certain level of reserves so that they remain sufficiently liquid. But they will definitely want them to have adequate capital to ensure that they remain solvent. Since the financial crisis of 2008, governments have been tightening such requirements.

A bank's capital is effectively its own savings. These derive from two main sources. The first is shareholders who have provided equity capital either when the bank was founded or as a result of subsequent share issues. The second is from retained operating profits. So if a bank started out with $100 million in shareholder funds and over the years accumulated profits of $20 million its total capital would be $120 million. A bank will need sufficient capital to ensure that it can survive if any of its loans go bad. The more loans it makes, the more capital it will need as a buffer against insolvency. Thus a regulator might insist on a simple capital ratio of 10 per cent. On

---

## Basel sets the capital rules

The Bank for International Settlements (BIS) is the world's most exclusive bank, since its only customers are national central banks. It was founded in 1930 in Basel, in Switzerland, partly at least because of its location: in those days, central bankers travelled by train and Basel had good connections with the rest of Europe.

The BIS hosts meetings and publishes research. But it also acts as a superbanker, a place where central banks can deposit some of their reserves. It can also act as a superlender of last resort when even the national lenders of last resort get into trouble. The BIS can organize a global whip-round from other central banks, which it has done on behalf of Mexico, for example, and Brazil.

Another important BIS function is to set global banking standards, such as indicating how much capital banks should maintain so as to offset losses from bad loans. Since 1988, these have gone through a series of iterations: Basel I, II, and III, each of which has tried to tighten things up further. Basel I divided capital into two tiers. Tier 1 consists of funds that have been contributed by stockholders, plus retained profits. Tier 2 adds some other types of capital which may not exist as ready cash – such as the increase in value of the bank's buildings since they were originally purchased. The amounts of capital can then be compared with the bank's 'assets'. In accounting terms, a loan you have made to another party is referred to as an asset, while any funds you have borrowed are classified as liabilities.

Basel II tried to apply a more sophisticated judgment of risk. This reduced the capital requirements for those banks taking lower risks. Basel III, from 2013, became stricter and, amongst other things, started to measure capital adequacy on the basis of a 'leverage' ratio. This is the ratio of Tier 1 capital to the bank's total assets – and is not risk weighted. Basel III suggested a leverage ratio of at least three per cent.

The Bank of England accepted this figure but requires more for the biggest banks, which could bring the total up to five per cent. Canada, which has the world's soundest banks, is implementing Basel III.

---

this basis, a bank with $120 million in capital would thus be able to make loans of up to $1,200 million. The actual rules can be a complex mixture of both liquidity and capital requirements. Such rules are established at the Bank for International Settlements. Since 2008, central banks have been trying to tighten up (see box).[5]

In addition, the G20 countries meet to consider these issues in the Financial Stability Board, which is charged with more general reforms of international financial regulation and with promoting international financial stability. In 2014 the Board introduced new rules for banks. On this basis, the 27 'globally systemic banks' have to hold buffers, referred to as total loss-making capacity, equivalent to 16-20 per cent of their loans. Just as important, if a bank gets into trouble it will not just be shareholders who lose out: bond holders, previously considered as creditors, will also take a hit. Another issue the Board is working on is 'living wills' to show how banks could be shut down in an orderly manner.[6]

If banks make a series of losses because of bad loans, they will either need to replenish their capital or reduce their lending. One way to get more capital is to issue more shares. Initially this means approaching existing shareholders for additional funds by offering them shares at a discount – a 'rights issue'. Then the bank can try to sell more shares to other institutions. In either case this may be difficult since the need to raise more capital can be interpreted as a signal that the bank is in trouble.

Countries differ in the way they apply such rules. In the US, banks are policed not just by the Fed, but by the Office of the Comptroller of Currency within the Treasury Department which is charged, amongst other things, with preventing money laundering and the financing of terrorism. In the UK, supervision of the banks has undergone a number of changes. From 1986 they were regulated by the Financial Services Authority.

## How we pay

Cash generally accounts for the greatest number of trans-actions, though its use is declining. In Australia, for example, between 2007 and 2013 the proportion of transactions carried out by cash fell from 69 to 47 per cent. Cash payments are generally smaller – so are a smaller proportion by value. The larger transactions are more likely to be carried out by check or online. In Australia, for example, cash transactions are 47 per cent by volume but only 18 per cent by value. In the UK the corresponding figures are 61 and 11 per cent[7], and in the US 40 and 14 per cent.[8]

Recent years have also seen a striking decline in the use of checks. Checks are disappearing in many countries: they were abolished in the Netherlands in 2001. The US lags in this respect: it has the highest number of transactions per person but is also one of the greatest users of checks.[9] The table below shows for selected countries the number of retail non-cash transactions per person. ■

| | Debit card | Credit card | Checks | Direct debits* | Direct credits | Total |
|---|---|---|---|---|---|---|
| United States | 165 | 84 | 58 | 42 | 28 | 377 |
| Sweden | 190 | 40 | <1 | 31 | 90 | 351 |
| Netherlands | 151 | 7 | 0 | 82 | 101 | 341 |
| Australia | 132 | 78 | 10 | 32 | 72 | 324 |
| Rep. Korea | 50 | 147 | 9 | 33 | 63 | 302 |
| United Kingdom | 129 | 35 | 13 | 54 | 58 | 289 |
| Canada | 126 | 90 | 22 | 20 | 28 | 286 |
| Belgium | 98 | 13 | <1 | 26 | 85 | 222 |
| Germany | 31 | 7 | <1 | 108 | 75 | 221 |
| Switzerland | 57 | 27 | <1 | 6 | 97 | 187 |
| Brazil | 20 | 24 | 7 | 22 | 46 | 119 |
| Italy | 18 | 10 | 5 | 10 | 21 | 64 |
| Saudi Arabia | 54 | 2 | <1 | <1 | <1 | 56 |
| South Africa | 26 | | 1 | 14 | 13 | 54 |
| Russia | 18 | 2 | <1 | 1 | 19 | 40 |
| Mexico | 8 | 5 | 3 | 1 | 9 | 26 |

Note: Direct debits refer to all electronic payments from bank accounts, not just specific direct debit mandates as used in the UK.
Source: RBA, 2014.

But this was considered to have been so ineffective during the financial crisis from 2008 that in 2013 it was abolished and replaced by the Prudential Regulation Authority and the Financial Conduct Authority, with some oversight by the Bank of England. In Canada, banks are regulated by the Office of the Superintendent of Financial Institutions and in Australia by the Australian Prudential Regulation Authority.

## From coins to illusions

Money has thus taken multiple forms – some of them useful, others illusory and capable of disappearing without even offering a puff of smoke. Banks, too, come in many different varieties. They include commercial banks, building societies, credit unions, investment banks, and many more, some of which are described in the next chapter.

**1** G Cooper, *The Origin of Financial Crises: Central banks, credit bubbles, and the efficient market fallacy* Harriman House, Petersfield, 2008. **2** Glyn Davis, *A History of Money*, Cardiff University Press, Cardiff, 2012. **3** David Graeber, *Debt: the first 5,000 years*, Melville House, London, 2014. **4** C Binham, 'RBS pays £390 million to settle Libor probe', *The Financial Times*, 6 February 2013. **5** H Benink and G Kaufman, 'Turmoil reveals the inadequacy of Basel II', *The Financial Times*, 27 February 2008. **6** 'Bank regulation: Buffering', in *The Economist*, 15 November 2014. **7** Payment Council. payyourway.org.uk/special-focus/payments-counter Accessed 30 December 2014, **8** B. Bennett, D Conover, S O'Brien and R Advincula. 'Cash Continues to Play a Key Role in Consumer Spending', *Fednotes*, Federal Reserve Bank of San Franciso, 29 April 2014. **9** RBA, *Payments System Board Annual Report – 2014*. Reserve Bank of Australia, 2014.

# 3 Banks of all shapes and sizes

From modest beginnings as the enterprises of Greek or Roman money-lenders perched on their benches, banks have evolved into many different beasts. Some, like credit unions or microcredit institutions, have strong and transparent links with lenders and borrowers. Others are much more obscure, such as the investment banks or shady offshore operations in tax havens that try to keep everyone in the dark.

THE TERM 'BANK' confusingly covers many types of institution, which can have very different functions. This chapter describes some of the principal types. If you are in a hurry, and are familiar with basic banking, you can skip this chapter. Or maybe it is worth checking again exactly who does what.

## Commercial banks

The best-known banks are the commercial, sometimes called retail or high-street, banks, which enable individual customers or businesses to establish current or savings accounts, or to take out personal loans or mortgages. While commercial banks provide many services, they make most of their profits by making loans.

Banking in the UK has become highly concentrated. Of the 16 clearing banks in 1960, 15 are now owned by one of the four big banking groups.[1] Indeed, it became even more concentrated after the 2008 financial crisis when the British government had to step in to bail out the Royal Bank of Scotland (RBS), Lloyds, Halifax Bank of Scotland (HBOS), Northern Rock and Bradford & Bingley. The government finished up owning 81 per cent of RBS and 39 per cent of Lloyds, though in 2014 it sold off the latter, reducing its stake to 25 per cent. It also sold the 'good' part of Northern Rock to Virgin Money but retained the

## The global behemoths

The table below lists the world's largest banks, ranked by their total assets – which are largely their loans. In recent years, banks in China have moved up the rankings; the Industrial and Commercial Bank of China has been in first place for three years in a row. Indeed, globally the drift has been to the east: between 2009 and 2015, the proportion of bank assets in Asia and Australasia rose from 28 to 38 per cent.[2]

*World's top ten banks, ranked by global assets, 2014*

| Rank | Bank | Country | Assets $ trillion |
|------|------|---------|-------------------|
| 1 | Industrial & Commercial Bank of China | China | 3.2 |
| 2 | HSBC Holdings | UK | 2.8 |
| 3 | China Construction Bank Corporation | China | 2.6 |
| 4 | BNP Paribas | France | 2.6 |
| 5 | Mitsubishi UFJ Financial Group | Japan | 2.5 |
| 6 | JPMorgan Chase & Co | US | 2.5 |
| 7 | Agricultural Bank of China | China | 2.5 |
| 8 | Bank of China | China | 2.4 |
| 9 | Credit Agricole Group | France | 2.3 |
| 10 | Barclays PLC | UK | 2.3 |

*Top 12 UK banks or building societies, ranked by UK assets, 2013*

| Rank | Bank | Assets $ billion |
|------|------|------------------|
| 1 | HSBC Holdings | 2,671 |
| 2 | Barclays | 1,346 |
| 3 | Royal Bank of Scotland Group | 1,028 |
| 4 | Lloyds Banking Group | 847 |
| 5 | Standard Chartered | 674 |
| 6 | NatWest[1] | 353 |
| 7 | Santander UK | 270 |
| 8 | Nationwide | 191 |
| 9 | Standard Life | 185 |
| 10 | The Co-operative Bank | 43 |

1. Subsidiary of the RBS group.
Source: Relbanks.com

*Banks of all shapes and sizes*

dodgy mortgages. In 2009, HBOS merged with Lloyds to form the Lloyds Group, which by 2013 held around 30 per cent of UK personal current accounts. But perhaps the sorriest tale in UK banking in recent years has been the fate of the Co-operative Bank (see box).

The size of the banking industry is a particular problem in the UK. Over the past 40 years, total assets of the banking system have risen dramatically. They rose from 100 per cent of gross domestic product to around 450 per cent – compared with 200 per cent in Japan, for example, and only around 70 per cent in the US. Much of this is because London has become a center for international banking. Around 30 per cent of the assets are of UK branches of foreign banks. The Bank of England has estimated that by 2050 the UK banking sector could be worth 950 per cent of the country's GDP.[3]

Compared with the UK, the situation in the US is more diverse. As of September 2014, there were 5,705 commercial banks.[4] Even here, however, many regional banks have failed or merged with other institutions. Banks have also been steadily consolidating in most

---

### The Co-op and the crystal Methodist

The Co-operative Bank was brought to its knees in 2013 by the incompetence of its board and particularly its chair, the Reverend Paul Flowers, whose predilection for cocaine had him dubbed the 'crystal Methodist'. The board took some disastrous decisions, notably to merge in 2010 with the Britannia Building Society, which tripled its size. The Co-op had been advised by investment bank JPMorgan Cazenove and accountants KPMG – who somehow concluded that the logic for the merger was 'compelling'. Moreover, encouraged by the government, the Co-op had also been planning to take over 632 branches of Lloyds that had previously belonged to the TSB. Britannia proved to be a poisonous acquisition – £14.5 billion ($23 billion) in losses in commercial real estate. The deal was subsequently described as 'breathtakingly destructive'.[5] In December 2013 the Co-op Bank had to be rescued by a group of US hedge funds which took a 70-per-cent stake.

---

other countries. In Australia, for example, the big four banks – Commonwealth Bank of Australia, Westpac, National Australia Bank and ANZ – have 80 per cent of deposits.[6] In Canada, the corresponding group is the big five: The Royal Bank of Canada, the Toronto Dominion Bank, the Bank of Nova Scotia, the Bank of Montreal, and the Canadian Imperial Bank of Commerce.

A similar pattern is evident in developing countries. Here too the state banks stepped in to lend after the crisis. In Brazil, for example, three of the main banks are government owned and now have 43 per cent of bank assets.[7] In Nigeria, the government had to rescue nine banks, four of which subsequently merged with other banks, bringing the number of commercial banks down from 24 to 21.[8]

## Building societies

In the UK and Australia an alternative to a commercial bank has been the building society. Building societies were first formed in the UK in the 19th century when groups of people came together to save funds to help each other buy houses. The idea was that each society would be wound up when the last member had secured their house keys. Eventually, however, many societies became permanent, with a rolling membership, and by 1900 the UK had 60,000 building societies – at least one in almost every town.

Building societies differ from commercial banks in that they are 'mutual' bodies. The depositors own the society and have rights similar to those of shareholders in a company. Building societies accept deposits, on which they pay interest, and lend money from those deposits for the purchase of a property which the borrower uses as security. This is the most typical form of 'mortgage', which derives from the French for 'dead pledge' – this sounds morbid but it simply means that the pledge dies when the mortgage is paid off. Although building societies specialized in mortgage lending, eventually they were able to offer many other banking services. Compared with banks, they are more restricted since they must get a certain proportion of their loan funds from depositors. In the UK they can also borrow funds from other banks or institutions in the 'money markets' but are forbidden by law from getting more than 50 per cent of their funds in this way.

Unfortunately, many building societies have now been converted to banks. In the UK in 1986 the Thatcher government allowed the societies to 'demutualize' – to convert to limited companies or be taken over by a bank, if 75 per cent of their members voted in favor. This proved too tempting for many members, who stood to gain thousands of pounds in cash or shares. In 1997, five building societies and one insurance company provided their members with windfall gains of around £35 billion ($58 billion).[9] Demutualization proved disastrous. Almost all the demutualized societies in the UK over-reached themselves, and any former members who retained the shares would have subsequently made dramatic losses. By 2014 there were only 46 building societies, though these were still responsible for 19 per cent of savings and household mortgages.

Many Australian building societies also disappeared in this way. One of the first to succumb was the NSW Building Society which in 1985 became Advance Bank Australia. In 1985 Australia had 66 building societies[10], but by 2014 the number was down to just six.[11]

## Savings and loan associations

In the United States the equivalents of building societies have been savings and loan associations, also called federal savings associations, or 'thrifts'. Modelled on their British counterparts, they too date back to the 19th century. For decades these were safe institutions, with deposits guaranteed by the government. At their height, following World War Two, there were about 6,000 thrifts, responsible for more than one-third of mortgages. At that point they were highly regulated: their deposit rates were fixed and they were confined to a limited range of mortgage-related activities.

But in the early 1980s the thrifts too were laid low by inept deregulation, which removed many of the previous restrictions but did not apply corresponding supervision. As a result, many thrifts, some of which were seized by fraudsters, started to gamble with high-risk loans and by the end of the 1980s were going bust. In 1989 the US government had to take over and close or reorganize 747 of them at a total cost to the taxpayer later estimated at around $147 billion. In 2014 there were only 460 government-regulated federal savings associations. However, to compete with other institutions, they have been operating more like commercial banks.

## Credit unions

Credit unions are similar to building societies in that they are forms of mutual saving. These are non-profit organizations, owned and controlled by their members on a one-person one-vote basis, and have often been established in places too poor or remote to have their own banking services. The worldwide credit union movement began in Germany in the 1840s. Unlike building societies, they appear to be expanding. Globally, between 1998 and 2013, the number of credit unions rose from 37,623 to 56,904 (see table page 48).[12]

Credit unions have the advantage for their members of giving more attractive lending and borrowing rates. In some communities they offer people's first experience of democratic control, and can promote development by ensuring that funds circulate locally. Credit unions are strongest in North America and the Caribbean, where the 'penetration' – the proportion of the population of working age who are members – is 46 per cent.

## Global credit unions

Between 1998 and 2013, the number of credit unions globally rose from 37,623 to 56,904. In total, they had 208 million members who had $1.4 trillion in savings and $1.1 trillion in loans.

### Credit unions worldwide

| Region | Countries | Unions | Members '000s | Penetration | Savings $ billion | Loans $ billion |
|---|---|---|---|---|---|---|
| Africa | 25 | 22,385 | 17,032 | 6% | 5 | 6 |
| Asia | 21 | 21,570 | 42,017 | 3% | 131 | 115 |
| Caribbean | 19 | 398 | 3,181 | 18% | 5 | 4 |
| Europe | 12 | 2,390 | 9,194 | 4% | 24 | 12 |
| Latin America | 15 | 2,540 | 23,967 | 7% | 40 | 40 |
| North America | 2 | 7,405 | 108,607 | 46% | 1,161 | 897 |
| Oceania | 9 | 216 | 4,935 | 21% | 67 | 61 |
| World | 103 | 56,904 | 207,935 | 8% | 1,433 | 1,135 |

Notes: World total includes small numbers in Central Asia and the Middle East. Penetration is the membership as a proportion of the population of working age.
Source: WOCCU, 2014

In Canada the credit unions, with around 11 million 'member-customers' and a penetration rate of 43 per cent, provide stiff competition to commercial banks. The first credit union was created in 1900 in Levis, Quebec, when 80 people banded together as a *caisse populaire*. Although, as a result of mergers, the number of Canadian credit unions has fallen, the membership has risen continuously, to 10 million. The largest of these is the Desjardins Group, based in Quebec, which is Canada's sixth largest financial institution, with assets over $200 billion, six million members and 2,270 branches or ATM stations.[13] Outside Quebec, as a result of mergers, the top 10 credit unions now account for

87 per cent of assets.[14] Credit unions are also strong in the United States, where there are 97 million members.

Credit unions have a lower profile in the UK. Penetration is only 2.8 per cent. In 2014 there were 375, with around one million members and £1 billion in assets. Typically they are strongest in Scotland, the largest being Scotwest, with around half a million members.

## Investment banks

Investment banks differ from commercial or high-street banks. The original investment bankers were often

---

### Local exchange trading systems

Another type of financial institution, though not a bank, and more common in developed countries, is a Local Exchange Trading System (LETS). This involves the creation of new money – though in a strictly local form. The idea originated in Canada in the 1980s and now exists in multiple variants across the world. Although there are no full estimates of the number of groups, the Community Exchange System, which offers them global online services, covers 728 groups in 72 countries. In addition, Australia has its own Community Exchange System server for over 50 groups.[15]

A LETS system is essentially a club through which people buy or sell goods and services but without using dollars or pounds or any conventional currency – quite handy if you do not have much. Instead, the club keeps a central register of transactions. You might, for example, offer to mow your neighbor's grass, in which case he or she will declare to the register that you should be credited with a certain number of units, which you could then spend on vegetables from another neighbor's allotment. The units can have any name but usually have some local reference: in Reading in the UK, for example, they are known as 'readies'.

Although some businesses will accept LETS currencies, most transactions are for personal arrangements, hobbies or pastimes. The great strength of LETS schemes is that they promote community organization – and also remind their members of the nature of money. In fact, LETS systems make new, if limited money, just as banks do, by creating credits in people's accounts. When those credits are cancelled out, the money disappears again.

---

merchants who, in the course of buying or selling, would lend money to suppliers or customers. Nowadays, investment banks provide a wide range of often obscure services to large corporations, governments and other financial institutions. Globally around half their fee income comes from advising companies engaged in mergers and acquisitions. Much of the rest comes from fees for helping companies wishing to issue shares, advising them on what the price should be in the initial public offering and guaranteeing or 'underwriting' the issue by volunteering to buy any shares that are not taken up.

In 2014 the world record initial public offering was set by the Chinese internet company Alibaba which, with the assistance of Credit Suisse, sold shares worth $25 billion. Later the company issued bonds worth around $8 billion in a sale managed by Morgan Stanley, Citigroup, Deutsche Bank and JPMorgan Chase.

Investment banks also have their own capital, initially provided by shareholders, which they can use to trade on their own account. This is more hazardous than managing other people's money. One of the oldest British investment banks, Barings, was ultimately ruined in 1996 by one of its traders, Nick Leeson, who was effectively gambling with the bank's money and lost heavily.

Although investment and commercial banks are different, they have often had a close relationship. Indeed, many institutions are now 'universal' banks that cover both functions. This is risky, since a failure in the investment banking arm could also bring down the commercial bank. So dangerous was this prospect that in 1933 the US passed the Glass-Steagall Act, which prevented commercial banks from owning investment banks. Many that had started out as investment banks and then developed retail services then had to split the two functions. After the act was repealed in 1999,

Citigroup and JPMorgan Chase, for example, moved back into investment banking.

Since investment banks are continually raising funds, they are always alert to potential deals. In 2011 Goldman Sachs, for example, raised funds for Facebook from private investors by selling a type of bond that the investors were later entitled to convert into shares. These lucky investors were able to double their money a year later when Goldman managed the sale of Facebook, valuing the company at $50 billion. In 2014 Goldman was planning a similar ruse for the controversial taxi app, Uber.[16]

## Banking casualties

The 2008 financial meltdown produced some spectacular casualties among the investment banks. They had been borrowing huge sums to trade on their own accounts, buying shares and other assets to take advantage of rising prices. In 2007 the five independent US investment banks had borrowed between 25 and 35 times the value of their shareholders' equity in order to gamble on the markets.[17] When the markets started to collapse, the lenders withdrew their funding, leaving the investment banks staring over a precipice.

In March 2008, the 85-year-old bank Bear Stearns imploded and, chaperoned by the US government, was bought by the universal bank JPMorgan Chase for next to nothing. In September 2008, another bank, Lehman Brothers, also got into deep trouble. This time, however, the government was less forgiving and, after trying to get Barclays to rescue it, decided to make an example of Lehman Brothers and let it go bust – owing a cool $613 billion and bequeathing the liquidator a rat's nest of transactions to unwind, making this the world's messiest ever bankruptcy. In the same month even the once-mighty Merrill Lynch scurried to the shelter of a universal bank by selling itself to Bank of America for $50 billion.

Since the crisis, investment banking has become less profitable. In 1999 the industry had revenues of around $342 billion but by 2013 this had fallen to around $250 billion, around half of which came from trading in bonds.[18] The largest banks in the US are JPMorgan and Goldman Sachs and in Europe Barclays and Deutsche Bank. To some extent the decline in their revenues reflects the overall economic downturn. But investment banks have also had to face tougher regulation aimed at making them less dangerous. Another factor is that many of their former activities, such as share trading, can now be automated – delivered 'through the box'.

## Offshore financial centers and tax havens

The largest commercial banks usually have branches in many countries. This is useful for customers who want to transact foreign business. But these banks may also have branches in small countries that have no significant trade – in what are called offshore financial centers (OFCs). In this case, however, their customers are generally looking for secrecy, politely referred to as 'discretion'. Such centers are not necessarily very far offshore. The UK, for example, has OFCs in the Channel Islands and the Isle of Man. Indeed, the UK is responsible in one way or another for a high proportion of OFCs since many, like Bermuda, the British Virgin Islands, or the Cayman Islands, are former colonies – and many are staffed by British expatriates.

Offshore centers are difficult to identify precisely. They may, for example, be thought of as places where most transactions are carried out by non-residents. But non-resident activity is not confined to dodgy Caribbean jurisdictions. The City of London is a huge offshore financial center in that many of its customers live overseas.[19] In fact the City is also at the center of a vast 'hub-and-spoke' system with money being pumped in and out from offshore centers. The UK and its offshore satellites channel one-third of all international investments. The European Union also offers a number of regulatory havens for various kinds of tax dodging across the EU.[20] The rock band U2, for example, has moved part of its music empire from Ireland to the Netherlands in order to pay less tax.[21]

Across the world there are thought to be 70 centers with significant offshore activities. Not all are tax havens, but most are. A tax haven, as defined by the Organization for Economic Cooperation and Development, fulfils four criteria: an almost total lack of direct taxation; weak local economic activities; impenetrable tax rules; and a lack of disclosure of information to the tax authorities of other countries. Tax havens are allowing the world's wealthiest people to stash away around $30 trillion. As they have avoided tax in their own countries, at a rate of, say, 30 per cent, it has been estimated that this would have funded public services in their home countries by an extra $190 to $200 billion per year.[22]

Offshore banks and companies are also useful for those engaged in illegal activities, particularly international organized crime and drug dealing, since tax havens are also ideal locations for money laundering. Criminals aiming to cloak the murky origins of their funds can set up webs of companies in multiple jurisdictions and transfer funds between various banks with different reporting requirements, making it hard to establish the electronic equivalent of a paper trail.

## Islamic banking

At the other end of the financial and moral spectrum are Islamic banks. According to sharia law, Muslims are forbidden from investing in unethical industries, such as liquor, gambling or pornography. Islam also requires its followers to use their wealth judiciously and not hoard it, and even forbids not just usurious rates of interest, but any interest at all.

This may appear a fatal restriction, but in practice Islamic banks achieve the same results through other means – generally by fudging the distinction between banking and investment and enabling customers to share profits and losses. If, for example, a customer wants a loan to buy a house or a car, the bank will buy the item and then resell it to the customer at a higher price, in instalments over an agreed period. The price difference corresponds to what other banks would charge as interest.

They take a similar approach for savings accounts. When a customer makes a deposit, the bank invests this directly in businesses and then shares the profits with the customer. For customers, this has a further merit: these businesses have to comply with sharia law and refrain from unethical activities. This mechanism is thus also attractive for non-Muslims who have similar moral scruples.

Globally this has become an increasingly important business. Between 2009 and 2013 it grew annually by 18 per cent. By 2014, Islamic financial products totalled around $2 trillion, mostly controlled either by Islamic banks or the Islamic sections of conventional banks and the rest in *sukuk*, which is the Islamic equivalent of bonds.[23] Never slow to sniff out a financial opportunity, the City of London has now become a center for Islamic financial services. Although London has been providing these for the past 30 years, it has now vastly increased its Islamic offerings through more than 20 banks. The British government has also got in on the act by issuing *sukuk* government bonds.

Deciding what is or is not compliant can be tricky. Islamic banks rely on boards of scholars who act as 'Islamic rating agencies' – for a suitable fee. At present, there is no final authority, though groups such as the Accounting and Auditing Organization for Islamic Financial Institutions are trying to establish global standards.

## Microfinance

Another distinctive and successful form of banking that has come to the forefront in recent years has been microfinance. Although many countries have traditionally had village savings and loan associations, the principles of modern microfinance were pioneered in Bangladesh from 1976 by Mohammad Yunus, who established the Grameen (village) Bank and won the 2006 Nobel Peace Prize for his achievements. The idea is simple. Poor people cannot usually get even tiny loans from banks because their business is too small and they can offer no security, no 'collateral'. Yunus realized, however, that the poor, and particularly women, were among the most careful users of money precisely because they had so little of it. He therefore replaced collateral with trust. In this type of microfinance scheme, women join together in small groups applying peer-group pressure. This can ensure strikingly high loan recovery rates – over 98 per cent. The borrowers can get microloans for productive self-employment, at close to market interest rates, repaying on a monthly or weekly basis. The women also have to make regular savings. Once the money is repaid, members can take further loans. The women also get training and other support, including help with their children's education.

In many microfinance schemes, borrowers gain access to funds through group lending so that if one member does not repay her loan, all the other members also suffer. The others may thus have to contribute to avoid being denied future loans. This represents a form of joint liability with a degree of self-screening, reducing the need for the lender to assess each individual closely – which helps bring down costs. A survey of 146 groups in Madagascar, for example, found that the groups that performed best were those with stronger mutual ties and clear internal rules and regulations.[24]

Thousands of other microfinance institutions have sprung up. In 2010, 3,652 microfinance institutions around the world reported reaching 25 million clients.[25] In the past, most were operated by non-governmental organizations, credit unions and other financial co-operatives or state-owned development banks. Grameen itself, however, came under pressure from the Bangladesh government, which in 2011 forced Yunus to resign and in 2014 effectively handed control to the Central Bank.

In recent years many commercial banks have spotted a profit opportunity and started organizing their own microfinance programs. This has created some controversy. Many people, arguing that it is immoral to make money out of the poor, say that microfinanciers should accept very limited profits. Others, however, particularly in Latin America, believe that it is important to involve profit-orientated private investors to ensure that sufficient capital is available.

Mexico's largest microfinance lender, for example, is Compartamos Banco, with more than 2.5 million clients. This was set up with just $6 million in capital, but when it went public in 2007 it raised $450 million for its backers. This could be because of the fairly extortionate rates it charges – around 100 per cent annually. Microfinanciers are now being called upon to sign a code of ethics, the Pocantico Declaration, designed to ensure that microfinance, while it should be a profitable business, should also be grounded on firm ethical principles.[26]

Another area of concern has been that microcredit does not really lift people out of poverty. However, an extensive study from the World Bank in 2014 seems to have put that issue to rest. It examined 20 years of microcredit in Bangladesh where, by 2011, there were 576 registered microfinance organizations. Around one-third of borrowers belonged to more than one

New kinds of financial institution are emerging in the form of computer networks that use 'virtual currencies'. Of these the largest is Bitcoin which was launched in 2009 by the mysterious Satoshi Nakamoto – though it has not been revealed who she/he/it/they is/are. Bitcoins are units of a virtual currency, also called a crypto-currency, created in a network of users' computers as a reward for doing some heavyweight number crunching. This is described as 'mining' and has been arranged such that ultimately only 21 million bitcoins can ever be mined.

Bitcoins then exist in a central register across the network which keeps track of each user's account, and payments can then be made by making transfers between one account and another. Bitcoins once mined also can be purchased outside the system for dollars and other non-virtual currencies in special exchanges. Bitcoins are analogous to 'fiat' money in that they have been created by a central authority, in this case a computer algorithm. They are also similar to local exchange trading systems in that all transactions are held in a central register. But they are also a form of commodity money since their value is ultimately determined by supply and demand.

Bitcoins, like gold, have the advantage of offering an international medium of exchange that avoids the need for foreign exchange markets. Unsurprisingly this also makes them attractive to drug traffickers and money launderers. But they have the corresponding disadvantage of fluctuating wildly in value. In late 2013, one bitcoin was worth $1,100 but by early 2015 it was worth only $200.■

scheme. The study found that those who borrowed achieved higher incomes and had more of their children in school.[27]

## The credit genie

Banking in all its forms has proved a remarkably profitable innovation. But once the credit genie is out of the bottle it can be difficult to control, opening up the prospect of bank failures and catastrophic collapse. But companies that want to raise funds do not rely only on banks; they can also issue shares and bonds. How this happens is the subject of the next chapter.

**1** Richard Davies and Peter Richardson, Vaiva Katinaite and Mark Manning. 'Evolution of the UK banking system', in *Quarterly Bulletin* 2010 Q4, Bank of England, London, 2010 **2** *World Financial Services Outlook*, Economist Intelligence Unit, Random House Business Books, London, 2014. **3** Oliver Bush, Samuel Knott and Chris Peacock, 'Why is the UK banking system so big and is that a problem?', in *Bank of England Quarterly Bulletin* 2014 Q4, Bank of England, London, 2014. **4** *Latest Industry Trends*, Federal Deposit Insurance Corporation, Washington, 2014. **5** A Brummer, *Bad Banks. Greed, Incompetence, and the Next Global Crisis*, Random House Business Books, London, 2014. **6** Australia, Country Financial Services Report, Economist Intelligence Unit, London, 2014. **7** Brazil Country Financial Services Report, Economist Intelligence Unit, London 2014. **8** Nigeria Country Financial Services Report, Economist Intelligence Unit, London 2014. **9** 'Demutualisation in Australia', *Reserve Bank of Australia Bulletin*, January 1999. **10** Ibid. **11** Customer Owned Banking Association, 2014, customerownedbanking.asn.au **12** *Statistical report*, World Council of Credit Unions, Madison, WI, US, 2014. **13** *Quick facts about Desjardins,* desjardins.com accessed 9 December 2014. **14** *System Results Sep 2014,* Credit Union Central of Canada, Toronto, 2014. **15** Community Exchange System, community-exchange.org accessed 9 December 2014. **16** Tom Braithwaite, Richard Waters and Tim Bradshaw, 'Goldman Sachs clients offered debt in Uber', in *Financial Times*, 1 December 2014. **17** 'Special report on international banking. Paradise lost', *The Economist,* 15 May 2008. **18** 'Twilight of the gods', in *The Economist,* 11 May 2013. **19** P McGuire and N Tarashev, *Global monitoring with the BIS international banking statistics*, BIS Working Papers No 244 by Monetary and Economic Department, 2008. **20** 'Not a palm tree in sight', *The Economist*, 16 February 2013. **21** 'Union berates Bono for supporting tax breaks for multinational corporations', in *The Guardian,* 12 October 2014. **22** *Tax us if you can*, Tax Justice Network, London, 2012. **23** 'Big interest, no interest', *The Economist*, 13 September 2014. **24** N Hermes and R Lensink, 'The Empirics of Microfinance: what do we know?', in *The Economic Journal*, 117 (February), F1–F10, 2007, Blackwell, Oxford, 2007. **25** Jan P Maes and Larry R Reed, *State of the Microcredit Summit Campaign Report 2012*, Washington DC. **26** R Blakely, 'Microfinance raises fresh sub-prime fears', in *The Times*, 14 July 2008. **27** Shahidur R Khandker and Hussain A Samad, *Dynamic Effects of Microcredit in Bangladesh*, Policy Research Working Paper 6821, Washington, World Bank, 2014.

# 4 Stocks, bonds and dodgy deals

The financial markets raise funds by issuing stocks and bonds. Governments, too, issue bonds to cover part of their expenditure – appearing to create alarming levels of public debt. But the real risks lie in the creation of arcane 'derivatives', the true values of which may be impossible to assess – and which place the world's financial system in jeopardy.

ALTHOUGH YOU EARN money as cash, if this accumulates you have to decide what to do with it. If you stuff banknotes under your mattress, you might feel on top of your finances. But in addition to risking burglary and some uncomfortable sleeping positions you could be wasting an opportunity because if you saved it in a bank you should be able to earn some interest, perhaps as much as five per cent per year. The mattress option also exposes you to the risks of inflation, because $100 withdrawn from your mattress could, one year later, be worth two per cent less in terms of goods you could buy with it than when you first earned it. In Canada, for example, between 2004 and 2014 inflation averaged 1.7 per cent per year. This means that over those 10 years the value of C$100 fell to C$81.[1] You will probably therefore choose to put your money in a bank where it will earn sufficient interest to overcome the effects of inflation.

The bank can afford to pay you interest because your deposits help it run more smoothly and profitably. However, this is not because it is lending out your savings. It creates loans out of thin air. The banks try to attract depositors for various other reasons, one of which is to ensure they have enough cash on hand to settle interbank transfers (see box page 60).

Usually as a saver you will get better interest rates if you can leave your money undisturbed for long periods.

If you want to be able to withdraw instantly you will be offered a lower rate than if you are prepared to give notice of one month, say, or one year. The extra notice gives the bank greater security, with less risk that they will suddenly run short of funds.

Of course, saving with a bank also brings risks. The bank itself could go bust if its borrowers reneged, and your money could then disappear with it. When deciding where to deposit your funds, you always have to balance income and security; generally, the higher the interest rate, the lower the security.

However, in the case of banks the risks for most depositors are quite low. The government will usually offer an official guarantee: either it will bail out the bank if it gets into trouble, or at the very least it will establish systems of deposit insurance that offer protection to small savers. The financial meltdown of 2008 had governments scurrying to increase the amount on which savers could rely. In the United States, the amount insured per depositor per bank is now $250,000. In Canada it is C$100,000 and in Australia A$250,000. The British government guarantees accounts up to £85,000. If you are in New Zealand, however, you are out of luck. The government has refused to offer such insurance on

## How banks use your savings

You might think that banks act as intermediaries between savers and borrowers – paying lower rates of interest to savers and charging higher rates to borrowers. In fact there is very little connection between the two functions. Banks do not use savings to make loans because they can simply create credit, and thus money, out of thin air. Their main constraints are the riskiness of the borrower, and the need to have sufficient capital available to soak up the damage should the borrower fail to repay.

So why does the bank also want your savings? If there were only one bank with a giant global monopoly it might not – since the person who took the loan could spend it with another customer of the bank, which could make corresponding adjustments to the two accounts. But actually, of course, there are hundreds of banks

Getting interest from your savings should help protect you from inflation. This graphic shows the difference in the UK between what is now called the minimum lending rate, set by the Bank of England, and the annual inflation rate. The rates for deposits in banks and building societies are typically one or two percentage points above the minimum rate. For almost all of this period, interest rates exceeded inflation rates, which was comforting for savers. However, following the financial crisis in 2008 the Bank of England slashed the rate to 0.5 per cent – way behind inflation. Any interest is better than none at all but in recent years savers have been having a tough time.

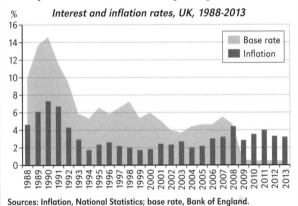

*Interest and inflation rates, UK, 1988-2013*

Sources: Inflation, National Statistics; base rate, Bank of England.

and millions of daily transactions between them. Often these payments just cancel each other out. But there are also likely to be fluctuations. Each bank could be a net recipient of funds one day and a net payer another. Your current (checking) and deposit accounts help to smooth out daily fluctuations – providing the resources to stabilize any volatility in the payments system. However, banks also encourage people to open current and savings accounts so that customers will treat them as a one-stop shop for their many profitable services.

It is worth emphasizing, however, that this way of operating is confined to licensed banks. The old-fashioned building societies, savings and loan associations and credit unions do not create money. They do indeed use savings to make loans. ■

the grounds that this will encourage risky behavior by the banks.

## Buy yourself a business

Depositing your money in a bank is of course only one way in which you can use your savings to earn money. You could instead buy a business such as a small shop. How much should you pay? You might think that all you need do is add up its various components: the value of the building, the fixtures and fittings and the stock. But it is unlikely that the owner would consider this fair. After all, the shopkeeper has done all the work of getting everything running smoothly and acquiring regular customers, so he or she would also want the price to reflect the fact that you would be buying a going concern. But how can you set a price on such imponderables?

The simplest way is to ask how much profit the business is earning. Let's assume it has a manager in place and all you would have to do is put up the funds and take the profits after all salaries and other expenses had been paid. According to her accounts, let's say the shop owner is making a profit of $50,000 per year.

How much would you be prepared to invest to earn that? If banks were offering a long-term interest rate of five per cent then to earn $50,000 in interest you would have to deposit $1 million – quite a lot. Should you pay $1 million?

Probably not. This is usually a riskier proposition than putting money in a bank. Lots of things could go wrong and you will have no guarantees. Generally, therefore, you would offer less, probably competing with other buyers who are also making similar judgments. Of course, you might think you could make the business even more profitable, by selling different goods, or by turning the prime location into a café. Nevertheless, the basic principle remains the same: you have to assess future profits and bid for the business accordingly.

### Equity options

As you probably don't have a million dollars to spare, or do not want the hassle of owning the whole business, you might prefer to buy only a part. The idea of selling shares in businesses has a long history. During the Renaissance, groups of merchants would get together to invest in the ships needed for particular voyages. But the first permanent business owned by shareholders was the Dutch East India Company in the 17th century.

Nowadays, starting a limited company involves issuing shares – as few as two. At the outset these are typically owned by the founder or the immediate family, or may be given to employees. Nevertheless, this is still considered a private company. In fact, many huge corporations are privately owned. Cargill, for example, which is one of the world's largest agribusiness corporations, is jointly owned by members of the Cargill and MacMillan families. And Mars, which supplies the world with Twix, M&Ms and Snickers – among other delights – is owned by members of the Mars family. In the US in 2014 there were 231 private companies that each had revenues of over $2 billion.[2]

In Europe one of the largest private companies is IKEA. Ingvar Kamprad, who founded the company, started out aged 17 in 1944 as a door-to-door supplier of nylon stockings and wallets. Through a byzantine collection of foundations and companies the Kamprad family still owns the business, which had revenues in 2013/14 of €28.7 billion ($32.4 billion).[3] Many companies prefer to remain private since they do not have to disclose many of the details of their operations, and can function more independently, perhaps with a longer-term vision.

Most of the larger companies, however, eventually choose to sell their shares to the public through a stock exchange. Perhaps the company needs to raise funds for expansion, or maybe the founders want to cash in on their success. At this point they will make an 'initial public offering'. For this purpose, the company will generally call on the services of an investment bank which, for a sizeable fee (one to two per cent), will advise the company on the initial share price and assist in the flotation. Usually this involves the investment bank putting its money where its mouth is by 'underwriting' the share issue – that is, it promises to buy any unsold shares – though it will normally disperse the risk by assembling an ad hoc syndicate. In 2014, for example, UK game company, King Digital, which makes Candy Crush Saga, raised $500 million with the help of Credit Suisse in a US share issue. In 2014, there were 1,206 initial public offerings, which raised a total of $257 billion.[4]

Once the company has gone public it then has substantial resources. It can use these to invest in a factory, for example, or to buy more raw materials. But a common option is to use the funds to swallow up competitors. Such takeovers are now common even in more sedate professions such as the law. In Australia, for example, law firms, which previously were partnerships, can sell shares to the public. One major firm, Slater & Gordon, went public in 2007 and within a year had used the funds to gobble up six smaller rivals. In 2012 it expanded to the UK where it bought three more law firms and by the end of 2013 had offices in Manchester, Liverpool, Sheffield and Halifax.[5]

### The share price barometer

The terms stocks and shares are often used interchangeably – 'shares' is generally used in the UK and 'stocks' in North America, but in both cases they are traded in stock exchanges. The term 'stock' harks back to 12th-century England, when transactions were recorded on hazel-wood tally sticks that were split in half – with one half, the stock, being taken by the creditor and the other half, the 'stub', being held by the debtor. Stocks and shares are also known as 'equities' and their prices can be very volatile since a company's perceived prospects can be shaped by many factors. Investors will consider not just its current profitability or the extent of its assets, but will also be swayed by rumors about future products, for example, or management changes. The share price is thus regarded as a barometer of company health.

As a shareholder you are now a part-owner and can vote for members of the board of directors. You are also entitled to any annual dividend. If the company makes a profit it can choose to distribute this to shareholders. On the other hand it may decide to retain the profits to invest in the business. In that case the value of the business, and thus the share price, should go up.

A business that sells shares gets the advantage of an injection of capital, but at the cost of a loss of control. A company that was happy to run itself for the benefit of its original owners or its workers, or even its customers, is now legally obliged to consider the views of share-holders – whose interests are often quite different. Shareholders are generally preoccupied with reaping annual dividends and seeing the value of their holdings rise. They are likely to fire directors, or through them, any managers whom they think are costing them money. Moreover, if the share price collapses, the company becomes ripe for a takeover. A low share price may allow a predator, often a competitor, to buy up a company very cheaply. The least popular purchasers, however, are the 'asset strippers' who will 'buy, strip and flip' a company – meaning that they sell off its assets at a substantial profit.

In practice, you are more likely to own shares indirectly. Around half of US publicly traded shares are owned by institutions, such as pension funds, and the rest by individual investors. In the UK, institutions are even more dominant, controlling more than two-thirds of listed shares.[6] Managing such funds is a huge business.

Insurance companies and pension funds have their own fund managers. But there are also funds which gather investments from individual, or 'retail', customers who pool these resources with other investors, into what in the UK are called unit trusts and in the US mutual funds. After the US, the UK is the world's second-largest center for asset management, looking after around $8 trillion in funds.

What do they do with this money? Firms such as Gartmore, PDFM, Schroders and Mercury in the UK put 70 to 80 per cent of their money into shares; two-thirds of this in the domestic market, and invest the rest in bonds or keep it as cash. Most of these funds claim to manage your money better than the average investor – that they will outperform the market. But of course all of them cannot. In fact, on average, they tend to do rather worse. Between 1984 and 2002, a period when the value of the top 500 companies in the US grew by 13 per cent a year, the average equity mutual fund returned only around 10 per cent.[7] For all the expertise they claim, success is mostly a matter of luck. Nevertheless, as long as the market is rising most will look vaguely competent.

Some will also reduce the risks of looking bad by not actively managing funds at all but simply by buying shares that match those in the standard stock exchange indices. By definition these passive 'tracker funds' should not be too disastrous. Moreover, they charge much lower fees. It has been estimated, for example, that someone who saved via a tracker fund rather than a high-cost managed fund would enjoy a 20-per-cent higher income in retirement.[8]

### Private equity

One of the most striking developments in recent years has been the emergence of predatory private-equity firms. These are enterprises which buy up other companies, either public or private, on the assumption that they can manage these firms better and eventually sell them on for a profit. Typically they do this by borrowing large sums from banks and then buying up all the company's shares, which are then removed from the stock exchange. Private-equity companies are usually themselves private companies, or owned by other financial firms – though the largest private-equity company, Blackstone, is a public company.

When a company takes over a business using borrowed funds, it is carrying out a 'leveraged buyout', anticipating that it can pay off the debt after it reorganizes and resells the company at a profit. In 2006, Blackstone carried out one of biggest-ever deals when it bought America's largest commercial landlord, Equity Office Properties, for $39 billion. This was less than the properties were worth, so within months Blackstone started to break up the company. By 2014 it had more than doubled the money it had invested.[9] Many private-equity operators have become fabulously wealthy. In 2014 Steve Schwarzman, the founder of Blackstone, earned $375 million and is now worth $11 billion.[10] Reportedly, he spent $3 million on his 60th birthday party, which included paying $1 million for a personal appearance by Rod Stewart.

## Selling bonds

Another way to raise funds for a business is to sell bonds. A bond is a financial contract in which the seller promises to pay the buyer a fixed rate of interest and, after a certain period, to repay the whole sum. The idea of bonds arose in the Middle Ages, when monarchs wanted to borrow large sums to finance wars. When they had run out of wealthy individuals they could tap, they divided their requests into smaller amounts by issuing bonds that could be bought by many other citizens. Some of the first bonds are thought to have been issued in Venice in 1157 to finance a war with Constantin-ople.[11] Bonds issued by governments are assumed to be very safe since governments cannot go bust in their own currencies – they always have the option of raising more taxes or printing more money.

Bonds issued by companies are inherently more risky, though when issued by large companies are normally considered 'investment grade'. Bonds were used, for example, to finance transcontinental railroads in the United States in the 19th century. Companies building infrastructure will sell bonds to help finance the huge upfront costs – and pay the interest and eventually the principal, using the income from fares and freight charges, for example. As with equities, bonds are usually issued on the advice of investment banks. Companies may sell the bonds directly to institutional or corporate investors. Or they may place them publicly, in which case they have to issue a prospectus which says what the funds are to be used for, when the bonds will be redeemed, and what rate of interest will be offered.

Corporations usually issue bonds that run from six to ten years. If they want money for shorter periods, up to three months, they issue an equivalent to bonds called 'commercial paper'. In the past, all bonds were issued as paper certificates and incorporated a set of coupons that could be torn off to collect each six-monthly payment. Nowadays most bonds are electronic transactions but the payment is still called a 'coupon'.

Bonds differ from shares in that generally they do not confer any control over the company. However, like shares, they can subsequently be bought and sold – in the bond market. And, just as with shares, the resale price can fluctuate. One reason for fluctuations is that the issuing corporation may get into difficulties and be considered a bad credit risk. But the main sources of volatility are changes in interest rates. To see why interest rates affect bond resale prices, suppose that at a time when interest rates are three per cent you buy a $1,000 ten-year bond from IBM which has a coupon, corresponding to an interest rate, of five per cent. That seems like a good deal – two percentage points higher than the prevailing interest rates. But interest rates fluctuate while the coupon on the bond is fixed. After a couple of years, interest rates might rise to six per cent, while your bond still has a coupon of only five per cent. This will make no difference to you unless you try to sell the bond. If you do, you will now find that it is worth less. If a potential buyer wanted to obtain a yield two percentage points above the prevailing interest rate, they would have to either buy a new bond with an eight-per-cent coupon or, to achieve the same result, they might offer to buy your bond for $620 – quite a drop. In this case the buyer will be considering the 'yield', which is the coupon divided by the current market price.

Of course the coupon, which is effectively the interest rate paid on the bond, is not the only factor, since the bond will eventually be redeemed for $1,000 and the closer you get to the redemption date the more you would get for it even at a time of high interest rates. Conversely, if interest rates fall then the market value of your bond goes up – and the company that issued it will be locked into paying a coupon which is higher than the prevailing interest rates. If you simply hang on to your bond you can ignore these fluctuations, safe in the knowledge that IBM will give you $50 per year and eventually return your $1,000 initial investment – though, after 10 years, inflation would have made this worth a lot less.

Corporate bonds typically have higher yields than government bonds. In 2014 the yield on a 10-year Treasury bond was around 2.6 per cent. For top-rated 10-year bonds issued by the major banks, the yield could be two percentage points higher. Unlike shares, bonds are not generally traded in exchanges but directly, either between buyers and sellers or via dealers in what are termed 'over-the-counter' trades. This means that the intermediaries, the bond dealers, stand to make huge sums from inside knowledge and contacts with other trusted dealers. However, we could now be reaching the stage where more bonds will be traded electronically.

### Junk bonds

Bonds are also issued by companies less solid than IBM. But since these bonds are considered riskier, such companies have to tempt buyers by offering higher coupons. Buyers who want to check on these bonds can consult credit-rating agencies such as Moody's or Standard and Poor's, which apply ratings – from AAA to CCC. In the past, around half the bonds rated CCC by these agencies have defaulted within six years. Bonds rated B- and below are considered 'high yield' or speculative, and are referred to as 'junk' bonds. In some periods, these have offered coupons eight percentage points above comparable investment-grade bonds.[12]

The ratings offered by the agencies are, of course, only their opinions, and they make mistakes. As elsewhere in financial markets, there is considerable margin for error – and consequently profit. In the past, the sellers of junk bonds have often been unnecessarily generous – or the buyers have been unduly skeptical. As a result, junk bonds have offered better yields than were merited by the actual risk.

Corporate bonds come in all sorts of varieties, which you probably don't need to know about. But just to give you a flavor, some – the 'callables' – allow the issuer to recall them before redemption, which is useful if interest rates fall. Others, the 'puttables', can be returned by the owner before maturing. Some have floating rates, while others, the 'zero-coupons' have no yield at all and instead are sold at the outset for prices less than the redemption rates.

### Asset-backed bonds

Most of these complexities are of interest only to bond traders, but one variety which is worth knowing a little about is the 'asset-backed' bond, since this was at the heart of the 2008 financial meltdown. This is akin to a share since, unlike a normal bond, in the event of default the owner has a degree of ownership, if not of the company as a whole at least of something that it produces or owns. One example is a mortgage bond. This is backed by property that could be sold off in the event of a default. Chapter 6 will explain in greater detail how this kind of insecure security triggered the financial crisis.

Investors who have the choice of buying equities or bonds face difficult decisions, as prices and interest rates change. But over the longer term equities have proved more profitable. Researchers at the London Business School estimated in 2007 that, over the previous century, investments in equities delivered four per cent more per year than bonds, which may not seem like much but eventually accumulates to a large sum.[13]

### Government bonds and national debt

The safest bonds to invest in are those issued by governments, particularly in the richer countries, which are good credit risks because they cannot go bust: if the worst comes to the worst, governments can pay back by raising taxes or just by printing more money. Government bonds, referred to as 'sovereign' debt, go under a variety of different names depending on the issuing countries. In the US, they are called treasuries, while in the UK they are called 'gilts' because originally the certificates had gilded edges. Local governments can also issue bonds, though these are typically backed by national authorities. In Canada, for example, each of the 10 provinces can issue debt to finance its own initiatives.

In the past, governments in developed countries often issued bonds to finance large infrastructure projects such as highways or bridges. If instead they had paid for such projects from current taxes, this would not only have been unpopular, it would also have meant charging people who might derive little benefit in their lifetimes. Raising the funds by selling bonds that would mature 20 or 30 years later would, by contrast, spread the burden and result in greater 'intergenerational equity'.

Nowadays, however, governments issue bonds primarily to balance the difference between income and expenditure – to finance a budget deficit. This accumulated deficit piles up as the 'national debt', which is held as bonds and other forms of securities by corporations, individuals, or within other parts of the government system.

Many people are alarmed at the scale of their national debts, and have issued public warnings – notably through digital National Debt 'clocks'. The original, which has been ticking since the early 1980s, is in Times Square in New York City. This clock can also be consulted online – for example, at nationaldebtclocks.org. If you are a US citizen and feel in a generous mood, the US Treasury invites public contributions to reduce the debt – please make your checks payable to the 'Bureau of the Public Debt'.[14]

Public debt can seem large. In the UK, for example, the national debt at the end of 2014 was $2.6 trillion – about $41,000 per person. Other countries also have significant per-capita debts: Australia, $17,000; Canada, $47,000; New Zealand/Aotearoa, $17,000; and the US, $45,000.[15]

Does this matter? Perhaps not. Public or 'sovereign' debt should not be assessed in the same way as personal debt – for which someone might knock on your door demanding repayment. Government debt issued as bonds in the national currency is not like that. Most of this is just money your government owes to its own citizens. So if you are a Canadian concerned that you owe $47,000, then just remember that you effectively owe a lot of that to yourself.

Most of this debt has been sold as bonds – 10-year, 20-year or 30-year. When the bond expires, the government can either pay this off, or 'roll it over' by issuing and selling another one. Most Western governments have little difficulty in selling bonds, particularly to pension funds and other institutions that need to invest a high proportion of their funds in safe assets. In the UK, pension funds have assets of around $2.7 trillion, which is of the same order of magnitude as the national debt – and the proportion is similar in other countries. They do not hold all of this as government bonds: in the UK the proportion is around 37 per cent.[16] In fact, arguably pension funds should be holding more of their assets as bonds rather than as risky stocks and shares.

The indebtedness of different countries can be compared to their gross domestic product – which is roughly the value of what the whole country produces each year. In the UK, for example, the debt is equivalent to 99 per cent of GDP; in Australia, 27 per cent; in Canada, 85 per cent; and in the US, 87 per cent. But it should be noted that this is not a percentage of GDP, and there is no particular significance to passing 100 per cent. The comparison is only intended to give a sense of scale.

If a country wants to reduce its debt, it can do so in a number of ways. One is to collect more in taxes than it spends on public services. It can then either buy back its bonds, or stop issuing new ones. This is what the Clinton administration in the US did around 2000. In this case, those who suffer will be the taxpayers. Or it can reduce the debt to GDP ratio by issuing debt more slowly than GDP rises. But ultimately the government can just print more money and use it to buy its bonds. This should lead to inflation. In this case the value of the currency will fall, so the people who will suffer will be the bond holders.

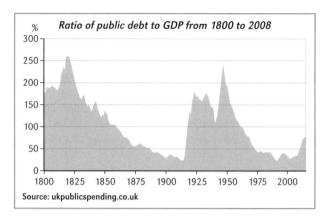

Ratio of public debt to GDP from 1800 to 2008

Source: ukpublicspending.co.uk

This may seem like an arcane discussion. But it can have very serious consequences. Among the key priorities of the rightwing Coalition government in the UK between 2010 and 2015 was to cut public services, which primarily hurts the poor, and also to cut taxes, which primarily benefits the rich. To these ends it focused attention on the rising national debt and argued for smaller budget deficits. This is a strange priority, since the national debt is not 'too high'. How would you know whether it was? One way would be to look at the historical pattern.[17] At around 100 per cent, the debt to GDP ratio in the UK at present is quite modest. In the past it has been two or three times as high.[18]

Another sign that government debt is not too high is that the bond markets say so. Indebted governments such as the UK have no difficulty in borrowing cheaply by selling bonds with redemption periods for decades into the future.[19] So why the panic? This is almost entirely political posturing and a pretext for imposing an ideological template. Surprisingly, governments that preach the value of market forces tend to ignore the markets when they give the 'wrong' answer.

As a result, the poorest people in many countries are

unnecessarily bearing the burden of swingeing austerity measures. Governments are cutting public expenditure, stifling economic expansion and punishing the poorest. The priority instead should be to create more wealth and distribute it fairly.

Bond issues often have different implications in the countries of the Global South. Rich countries have the advantage that many investors will happily buy their bonds – safe in the knowledge that governments ultimately cannot go bust because ultimately they can just print more money. But many developing countries do not have that option. They can certainly issue bonds in their own currencies but, with relatively small pension funds, they will find few local buyers. Most have indeed sold bonds to their national companies or institutions and so have accumulated some domestic debt. If these bonds are in the national currency, this is less of a problem.

But because their currencies are weak, and their credit records shaky, governments and companies in the Global South often issue bonds in other currencies, usually dollars. This means that they have a debt in a foreign currency, which is much more risky. If they have sold bonds for dollars and the local currency collapses, the government will find it difficult to obtain the currency to keep up the payments, or to reschedule the bonds, since it cannot print dollars. This is what contributed to the global debt crisis of the 1990s. Much of this was eventually resolved as a result of international campaigns. Around $130 billion-worth of debt for 35 countries was cancelled through the Heavily Indebted Poor Countries Initiative. Nevertheless, in 2014 a number of countries were still seriously in debt, including Jamaica, El Salvador, Pakistan, Tunisia and the Philippines.[20]

Public debt need not be a problem but private debt is another matter. The 2008 financial crisis had its roots in over-borrowing and over-lending in the US mortgage market. This triggered a collapse in a number of financial institutions that were themselves also overextended. If you worry about government debt in the UK at 99 per cent of GDP, bear in mind that the debts of financial-sector companies in 2011 were more than 800 per cent of GDP.[21]

## Derivatives

Thirty years ago bonds were considered safe investments, but rather dull. Now buyers have a Ben and Jerry's array of bond flavors to choose from. And traders with high-powered computers can use complex mathematical models to exploit minuscule differences in the yields of similar bonds. This is far more exciting. Much of the 2008 crisis arose, however, not as a result of trading directly in shares or bonds, but in what are termed 'derivatives' – contracts that are derived from, or based on, shares or bonds or some other financial instrument. While stock markets generally have been likened to casinos, the use of derivatives ratchets up the betting element to new heights.

Some derivatives take complex and bizarre forms, known as 'exotics', but others are relatively straight-forward. The simplest include 'futures', which allow buyers or sellers to buffer themselves against future price changes by locking their transaction to current prices. Companies often worry that, given they have to make long-term production plans, the prices of what they buy or sell will subsequently turn against them. If so, they can enter into a futures contract which enables them to buy or sell something at a later date but at a price that is fixed now. Futures trading has a long history. In the 16th century, for example, fish dealers in Holland were buying and selling prospective catches of herring. But by the 19th century this had developed into standardized contracts after the Chicago Board of Trade introduced futures trading in grain.

Nowadays airline companies, for instance, use futures to buy aviation fuel. Instead of just buying it on a daily basis, they enter into a contract to buy fuel at a certain price, say three or six months hence. At times this has served them well. During 2008, for example, some airlines were hedged at around $80 per barrel of oil. The actual price peaked the next year at over $150. In 2014, as the price fell to around $80, many airlines started to 'lock in', though when the price then continued to fall they may well have regretted this.

If you buy a future you are obliged to purchase the item on the due date, or to sell it to someone else. But you can also buy an 'option', which gives you the right, but not the obligation, to buy or sell something at a specific price in the future. Whether or not you exercise the option, you still have to pay up front for the privilege – which might add between 10 and 20 per cent to the final price.

Other derivatives involve various kinds of exchange known as 'swaps' (see box), among the riskiest being a 'credit default swap', which ..played a major part in the 2008 financial meltdown (see box page 78).

When used in moderation, futures and other

---

### An interest in swapping

Swaps seem rather unlikely derivatives but are used quite frequently. A common one is an interest-rate swap. One company which has a 10-year loan at a fixed interest rate could swap this with another company that has a similar loan but at a floating interest rate. Through a swap contract each would agree to pay the other's interest charges. Why would anyone want to do this? Generally it is because the two parties know more about each other than does the market. If, for example, a US company wants to expand in Europe, where it is not well known, and needs a loan in euros, it may have to accept one from a European bank at an unfavorable floating rate. It may therefore make a swap with a French company that is in a position to negotiate a better, fixed rate.

---

derivatives work like insurance policies. Many companies or institutions, nervous about market volatility, will buy or sell derivatives to protect or 'hedge' themselves. However, other companies – which have no need of, say, barrels of oil, or pork bellies – use derivatives primarily as vehicles for speculation. This is a high-risk occupation, particularly for sellers who do not actually own the item. Normally to buy a 'future', for example, the buyer needs only to deposit a part, perhaps 10 per cent, of the final payment; so for relatively small sums buyers can expose themselves to very large losses – or gains.

As a result, the volume of trading in derivatives far exceeds the trade in the underlying commodity. For while there is a limit to how much wheat is available, for example, there need be no limit to the number of futures contracts based on its price. Many of these contracts are

---

### Gambling with risk – speculating with credit

This is one of the newest forms of derivatives, though it is less obviously a swap and more a kind of insurance policy for holders of bonds or other volatile assets. The coupon on a bond, for example, is based on two considerations. The first is the prevailing interest rate in the market; the second is the risk that the company that sold the bond will go bust. The dodgier the company, the higher the risk component and thus the higher the coupon rate. A more cautious lender can pay someone else to remove the risk of default, for an annual premium – a 'credit default swap' (CDS). Companies selling this insurance may indeed be insurance companies, but banks and other institutions also sell CDSs. Note that this does not remove the risk entirely, since the insurance company itself could also go bust – a hazard known as 'counterpart' risk.

Suppose you have bought $10 million worth of bonds from Transnational Airways Inc that have a yield of five per cent – earning you $500,000 per year. Instead, you could have bought government bonds with a yield of only two per cent. This means that you are being rewarded for the risk element in Transnational to the tune of three percentage points.

But then you get cold feet. You could either rush off and sell

---

written by speculators who may be praised for providing a valuable service to those who really do need to hedge their position – or condemned as unproductive parasites who are exploiting the markets through their reckless gambling. Take your pick.

## Hedge funds

Much of the speculative trading in derivatives is carried out by 'hedge' funds. These were originally a means of hedging against the risk of sudden market slumps. Nowadays this is a serious misnomer since these funds are used not for achieving security but for high-stakes speculation. You can think of hedge funds as mutual funds for the rich. In the US, hedge funds will not let you through the front door unless you are prepared to invest at least $1 million and can demonstrate an income of more than $200,000 per year. Some will also lock

---

the bond or you could just sell the risk element, say to the Acme Insurance Corp. At three per cent of $10 million that would cost you $300,000 per year. If Transnational Airways remains in financial good health and continues to pay the coupon throughout the life of the swap contract, then nothing happens. Acme simply pockets the premiums, just as it would for any other policy for which a claim is never made. If, on the other hand, Transnational crashes to earth, then Acme has to pay you $10 million – though you still lose your premiums.

But that is much too simple. Speculators have seized on the credit default swap as a means of betting on the fragile financial health of Transnational Inc. Anyone can buy insurance on Transnational's bonds, whether they own them or not. Acme is happy to sell such CDSs to all comers. If Transnational goes bust, then those who do actually have the bonds will get their full value. Speculators who do not have any actual bonds still get paid, but not the $10 million. If, as a result of the bankruptcy, Transnational's bonds are being repaid by the liquidators at only 30 per cent of their value, then all you can claim from Acme is $7 million. Research suggests that all of this speculation actually makes it more likely that the target company will go bankrupt.[22]

up your money for five years. By the end of 2014, such funds were managing $2.9 trillion in assets.[23]

Typically they work on a very lucrative '2 and 20' basis, charging investors around 2 per cent of the assets managed, but also taking a 20-per-cent cut of any profits. This can make managers very rich. In 2013, the top 25 hedge fund managers between them earned $24 billion.[24]

Hedge funds follow a variety of strategies. Unlike mutual funds, which aim just to keep ahead of the market, hedge funds aim for much higher 'absolute returns'. And while mutual funds usually only gain good returns in a rising market, hedge funds can also make money in falling markets. They do this by 'shorting' shares they think will fall in value. This involves selling shares they do not actually own. Instead they 'rent' the shares, perhaps from a pension fund, sell them at their current price, and buy them back later, hopefully at a lower price, so they can hand the same number of shares back to the owner. If the share price goes up, however, they will lose. In one version called 'naked short selling' the speculators may not even borrow the stocks but sell shares they do not own by taking advantage of the grace period between when they sell the stock and when they have to deliver it – selling before buying.

There can be disastrous consequences for the companies whose shares they target. Once hedge funds smell blood in the water, their short selling can drive even potentially viable companies into a downward spiral. To protect the markets, the European Union applies restrictions to short selling. The US has banned naked short-selling altogether.

In addition to short selling, hedge funds may also engage in frantic trading, sometimes using computers to make instant automated trades. These quantitative funds – the 'quants' – may, for example, tell the computer to watch for tiny variations in the price of the same stock in London and New York, or make assessments based on standard indicators of past and present performance. This can be hazardous, especially when a herd of computers using similar software and data all press their own 'sell' keys simultaneously and dump vast quantities of the same stocks onto unsuspecting markets.

Hedge funds do not just use the funds from their investors to rent shares; they also borrow huge sums from the money markets. If you make a profit of five per cent on a $1-million deal this will net you only $50,000. Hardly worth getting out of bed for. But if, for the same deal, you have also gathered from investors a further $10 million, then the profit to be shared with the investor will be around $500,000. This way of amplifying returns with borrowed funds is termed 'leverage'. Investors expect their funds to be leveraged in this way in order to achieve high profits. Of course, the corollary is that if the outcome is a five-per-cent loss, then you will lose $500,000. Indeed, when things go wrong, they do so in spectacular fashion. In traders' parlance, such funds 'eat like chickens, but shit like elephants'.

Investing in hedge funds is not for the faint-hearted. Governments assume that people putting their money in hedge funds know what they are doing, and so do not apply the same regulatory standards as they would for a company dealing with consumers. In the UK, hedge funds are not allowed to advertise to the general public.

In any case, you would probably be well advised to steer clear. If you were in the US and you held a conservative portfolio made up of 60 per cent shares and 40 per cent government bonds, then between 2004 and 2014 you would have beaten the average hedge fund.[25]

## Sovereign wealth funds

Another striking development on the global financial scene in recent years has been the emergence of 'sovereign wealth funds'. These are funds controlled by governments that have amassed surplus money which they want to invest beyond their own shores. This rings all sorts of alarm bells. If you are nervous about seeing local companies bought up by foreign transnationals, how about having them controlled by foreign governments such as those in Russia, or China or Saudi Arabia, which may manipulate your national companies for their own political purposes?

Globally, sovereign wealth funds control around $2.9 trillion in assets and are growing rapidly. The 10

## Top 10 sovereign wealth funds 2014

Sovereign wealth funds are investment funds controlled by governments that have amassed surplus funds which they want to invest overseas. In 2014, the main sovereign wealth funds between them controlled around $7 trillion in assets.

| | Fund | Country | Assets – $ billion | Source |
|---|---|---|---|---|
| 1 | Government Pension Fund | Norway | 893 | Oil |
| 2 | Abu Dhabi Investment Authority | UAE – Abu Dhabi | 773 | Oil |
| 3 | SAMA Foreign Holdings | Saudi Arabia | 757 | Oil |
| 4 | China Investment Corporation | China | 653 | Non-commodity |
| 5 | SAFE Investment Company | China | 568 | Non-commodity |
| 6 | Kuwait Investment Authority | Kuwait | 548 | Oil |
| 7 | Hong Kong Monetary Authority Investment Portfolio | Hong Kong, China | 400 | Non-commodity |
| 8 | GIC Private Ltd | Singapore | 320 | Non-commodity |
| 9 | Qatar Investment Corporation | Qatar | 256 | Oil and gas |
| 10 | National Social Security Fund | China | 202 | Non-commodity |

Source: Sovereign Wealth Fund Institute – swfinstitute.org/fund-rankings

largest are indicated in the table.[26] Where does all this money come from? Most of the older funds, such as those in the United Arab Emirates (UAE), Norway, Saudi Arabia, and Kuwait, are accumulated oil revenues. Countries concerned that they are exhausting natural resources put some of the proceeds into these funds as ways of saving for future generations.

This is also the case for smaller funds such as Canada's Alberta Heritage Savings Trust Fund, and the US's Alaska Permanent Fund. Others are 'stabilization funds' which the exporting countries use to smooth the impact of volatile commodity prices. Others, including those of China and Singapore, are derived from trade surpluses. Ironically, some of the funds – in Malaysia and Australia, for example – were established with the proceeds of privatizations, so while the state may have been selling assets at home it has actually been part-nationalizing foreign companies.

Sovereign wealth funds have been around for a long time – the Kuwait Investment Fund, for example, was established in 1953. For decades these funds did not attract much attention, operating quietly and often in secrecy. This was largely because most were controlled by regimes friendly to the West. Indeed, generally their investments were welcomed since they were recycling money back to the oil purchasers, who were only too pleased to see their money return. Attitudes started to change when Russia established its stabilization fund in 2003 and China set up its Investment Corporation in 2007. It was thought that these upstarts were less likely to play by the rules of Western countries.

Where do they invest their money? Much of it goes into various banks and funds. The larger sovereign wealth funds in the Gulf and China, for example, invest in Blackstone's property funds. But the portfolios are vast and diverse. Qatar owns the Harrods department store in London, as well as the French football club Paris

Saint-Germain. In 2014, the two Singapore funds GIC and Temasek invested in the Brazilian online sports apparel retailer Netshoes. [27]

A number of Western countries worried that these funds would start to buy up key strategic assets or use their financial muscle to exert political influence on Western companies and governments. The European Commission introduced a code which requires sovereign wealth funds to declare where their money comes from and what they are doing with it, and to promise to avoid using investments for political purposes.[28]

But there is one sovereign wealth fund at least that makes no secret of its political agenda. The Norwegian fund, which owns one per cent of the world's stocks, is known for its ethical stance. A panel of experts evaluates the 7,000 or so companies it holds shares in and recommends disinvestment if required. One of its most notable decisions was to pull out of Wal-Mart because of the company's poor record on labor rights in developing countries, where it used exploitative sub-contractors.

In recent years, however, most governments have become more relaxed about sovereign wealth funds. The government in the UK, for example, which is the most attractive destination for sovereign Gulf money, largely investing in property, is also considering setting up its own fund for investing government pension funds.

## Into the shadows

The capitalist system has thus devised ever more sophisticated ways of linking savers and borrowers – and allowing each to profit from the other. Indeed, the plethora of non-banking intermediaries constitutes what is now termed the 'shadow' banking system. This is a fairly vague term, but it includes hedge funds, various forms of mutual funds and, more recently, internet crowdfunding websites and other forms of peer-to-peer lending. These enterprises can offer services similar to those previously provided by banks. In 2013 the global shadow banking industry was estimated to be providing around $75 trillion in funds – though on a narrower definition the figure is around $27 trillion.[29] These institutions are much more lightly regulated than banks.

As the world's financial systems become more complex, they are also becoming less stable and more vulnerable to external events and to changes in mood and opinion. With appropriate regulation these risks may be partly manageable at the national level. But nowadays all financial systems are linked with those in other countries. The next chapter explores this mutual dependence, by looking more closely at systems of foreign exchange.

**1** *Inflation calculator*, Bank of Canada, 2014, bankofcanada.ca **2** Andrea Murphy, *America's Largest Private Companies* 2014, nin.tl/biggestUSfirms2014 accessed 10 December 2014. **3** Richard Milne, 'Ikea sales growth accelerates as consumer confidence improves', *Financial Times*, 13 September 2014. **4** Andrew Bolger, 'IPO market set to fall short of expectations', *Financial Times*, 10 December 2014. **5** John Hyde, 'Slater & Gordon confirms another UK acquisition', in *Law Society Gazette*, 24 October 2013, nin.tl/oztakeover **6** M Bishop, *Essential Economics*, Profile Books, London, 2009. **7** 'The law of averages', *The Economist*, 3 July 2003. **8** 'Against the odds, in *The Economist*, 22 February 2014. **9** Henry Sender, 'Blackstone hunts for Reits it can take private', *Financial Times*, 1 December 2014. **10** '400 richest people in America', *Forbes* online, forbes.com **11** M Levinson, *Guide to Financial Markets*, London, Profile Books, 2006. **12** *Financial Centres, Canada*, Economist Intelligence Unit, London, 2008. **13** 'Clare and present danger', *The Economist*, 6 November 2008. **14** US Treasury, 2008, nin.tl/USdebtfaq **15** 'The global debt clock', *The Economist*, 2014, nin.tl/globaldebtclock accessed 11 December 2014. **16** *Global pensions assets study*, Towers Watson, 2013, towerswatson.com **17** *Paying off government debt: Two centuries of global experience,* Global Financial Data, 2014, https://globalfinancialdata.com **18** ukpublicspending.co.uk **19** 'Government debt: How much is too much?', *The Economist*, 2 January 2013. **20** Jubilee Debt Campaign, 'Election 2015: How to avert a new debt crisis', jubileedebt.org.uk accessed 12 December 2014. **21** Douglas Sutherland, Peter Hoeller, Rossana Merola & Volker Ziemann, *Debt and macroeconomic stability*, OECD Economics department working paper no 1003, OECD, Paris, 2012. **22** G Marti, G Subrahmanyam, Dragon Yongjun Tang & Sarah Qian Wang, 'The Effect of Credit Default Swaps on Credit Risk', *Review of Financial Studies*, 27, 2927-2960, 2014. **23** 'Can't pay, won't pay', *The Economist*, 20 September 2014. **24** Matthew Vincent, 'Investing in event-driven hedge funds looks like a lose-lose strategy', *Financial Times*, 4 December 2014. **25** 'Can't pay, won't pay', *The Economist*, 20 September 2014. **26** A Blundell-Wignall, Yu-Wei Hu & J Yermo, 'Sovereign Wealth and Pension Fund Issues', *Financial Market Trends*, OECD, Paris, 2008. **27** Jeremy Grant, 'Singapore leads the pack in sovereign wealth deals', *Financial Times*, 3 November 2014. **28** Fred Halliday,. 'Sovereign Wealth Funds: power vs principle', openDemocracy, 5 March 2008, nin.tl/stolenwealthfunds **29** *Global Shadow Banking Monitoring Report 2014*, Financial Stability Board, London, 2014.

# 5 Dollars without borders

Money is available all over the world with a few taps on an ATM machine. But if your home account is in Australian dollars, and you are in Mexico or Thailand, how many pesos or baht will you get? This will depend to some extent on the strength of the Australian economy. But the value of any currency can also swing wildly if it comes under speculative attack. In self-defense, some countries have come together to share a currency. Others have thrown in the towel and adopted the money of another country, often the US dollar.

In an era of globalization, we are well aware of how countries have become more financially interdependent. A crisis of confidence in New York will inevitably be followed by jitters in London, Frankfurt, Hong Kong and Tokyo – and will be reflected in fluctuating share prices or stuttering demand for commodities or consumer goods. One of the most direct indicators of the shifting balance of financial power is expressed through currency exchange rates.

The earliest international traders did not worry much about exchange rates. Either they bartered with their trading partners – swapping manufactured trinkets, perhaps, for spices or furs or exotic foreign silks – or they could use gold or silver. But as trading activity increased, so too did the use of national currencies. Traders arriving in fifth-century Athens, for example, would have to obtain local currencies from money-changers who would set up their tables in the marketplace. In modern Greek, the word *trapeza* means both a table and a bank.[1] Even when both currencies used gold coins, traders generally felt more comfortable working with the local currency since they might not trust strange foreign coins.

One millennium and a half later, the international flow of currencies is not just vastly greater but increasingly frenzied. In 2013, the world's foreign-exchange markets bought and sold, on average, $5.3 trillion dollars-worth every day.[2] You might think this just reflects the need to buy and sell goods across international frontiers, but in fact it is around 35 times greater than the flow of international trade.[3]

## The value of currencies

What determines the relationship between one currency and another? What is one euro, or one dollar, or one rupee actually worth? Ultimately what matters is what it will buy. To assess their comparative values, you might look therefore at what it costs to buy the same commodity or item in different countries. This is not as simple as you might think, since across the world people buy different things. Even the most basic foods have many grades. Rice, for example, has around 7,000 varieties – from basmati rice in India to jasmine rice in Thailand. So assessing currencies according to how much rice they will buy in each country could lead you astray.

What is needed, therefore, is something for which there is a clear international standard. *The Economist* magazine has a not entirely serious, but instructive, point of homogenized reference – the McDonald's Big Mac, an item produced to the same relentless recipe in around 120 countries. In the US in July 2014 the Big Mac cost $4.80 and in Colombia the same item cost 8,600 pesos, so you might guess that the exchange rate could be arrived at by dividing 8,600 by 4.80, which would make it around 1,794 pesos to the dollar. Assessing currencies in this way, according to what they will buy in each country, is referred to as using 'purchasing power parity' (PPP). In fact, for the Colombian peso the value suggested by the Big Mac is similar to that in the foreign-exchange markets: in July 2014 the rate was 1,848 pesos to the dollar.[4] There has also been a reasonable correspondence for other currencies, such as the Australian dollar or the Indian rupee (see table).

For other currencies, however, the two assessments are some distance apart: in the case of the Argentinean peso, for example, by a factor of two. This might suggest that there is something wrong with the Big Mac index – a fundamental flaw in 'burgernomics'. One issue is that the price of the burger will depend not only on its ingredients, which are common and mostly traded internationally, but also on things for which prices are set locally, such as wage costs or rents, which are likely to be quite different in New York or Oslo or Kolkata. The other

### 'Burgernomics'

To assess the comparative values of currencies, you might look at what it costs to buy the same thing in different countries. *The Economist* magazine has a useful point of reference – the McDonald's Big Mac, which is produced using the same formula in around 120 countries.

*Big Mac index, 2014*

| Country | Currency | Big Mac in local currency | Implied exchange rate | Market exchange rate |
|---------|----------|---------------------------|-----------------------|----------------------|
| United States | $ | 4.8 | 1.0 | 1.0 |
| Australia | A$ | 5.1 | 1.1 | 1.1 |
| Brazil | Real | 13.0 | 2.7 | 2.2 |
| Britain | £ | 2.9 | 0.6 | 0.6 |
| Canada | C$ | 5.6 | 1.2 | 1.1 |
| China | RMB | 16.9 | 3.5 | 6.2 |
| Egypt | E pound | 16.9 | 3.5 | 7.2 |
| India | Rupee | 105.0 | 21.9 | 60.1 |
| Japan | Yen | 370.0 | 77.2 | 101.5 |
| New Zealand | NZ$ | 5.7 | 1.2 | 1.2 |
| Russia | Rouble | 89.0 | 18.6 | 34.8 |
| South Africa | Rand | 24.5 | 5.1 | 10.5 |

Source: Economist, 2014

*Dollars without borders*

possibility is that the markets are pricing currencies on things other than their local purchasing power.

A more sophisticated approach extends the purchasing power parity method beyond Big Macs to embrace a more extensive 'basket' of goods. This is used as the basis of international statistics comparing the cost of living between different countries (see box).

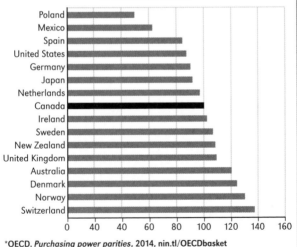

## Work in Switzerland, spend in Poland

The Organization for Economic Co-operation and Development (OECD) has calculated for many countries how much it would cost in their own currency to buy the same basket of goods in many other countries at prevailing exchange rates. The results are shown here for Canadian dollars. The same basket of goods that would cost C$100 in Canada would cost only C$49 in Poland but C$138 in Switzerland. This shows how the relative value of currencies is set only partially by what they will buy. As a result, the cost of living can vary greatly between one country and another.

*Comparative price levels around the world in Canadian dollars*

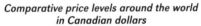

*OECD, *Purchasing power parities*, 2014, nin.tl/OECDbasket

In practice, currency dealers are often less interested in the fundamentals of what currencies are really worth and more concerned about how exchange rates will move today or tomorrow. In this case, it is simpler to consider currency prices in terms of supply and demand. The demand for dollars will go up if people in Australia, for example, need US dollars to buy US goods, or invest in US companies, or buy US treasury bonds. Rising demand for these will push up the value of the US dollar. On the other hand, if US consumers or companies want to import more from Europe or Asia, they will have to exchange their dollars for other currencies, and this will tend to depress the value of the dollar. Similar trade and investment takes place across over one hundred countries – setting market prices for currencies based on supply and demand.

In addition, you can get a price not just for selling euros or rupees now but also for doing so in three months' time, or up to one year ahead. Just as you can buy futures in wheat or coffee, so you can buy futures in currencies. This is useful for exporters who will be paid for their goods in a foreign currency and want to 'lock in' their income.

## Governments intervene

A further consideration is government activity. Generally speaking, individuals and companies in the UK, for example, will not hold dollars for very long. If they do not spend them on buying goods from the US or to invest in the US they will sell their dollars for pounds. The British government, however, via the Bank of England, may well want to keep stocks of foreign currencies to add to its reserves of dollars or yen or euros. It uses these reserves for various purposes. One is to buffer short-term fluctuations in trade or investment – as exports or imports rise and fall from month to month, the Bank will have the flexibility to add to or draw from its currency reserves to avoid unnecessary fluctuations in exchange rates.

Governments can also deploy their foreign-currency reserves to influence exchange rates. The Bank of England, for example, might consider that the pound is temporarily undervalued – which would make imports more expensive than necessary and provoke inflation. If it has sufficient reserves of dollars or other currencies it can use these to buy pounds – which should increase the demand for pounds and thus push the exchange rate up.

In addition, governments can influence exchange rates by altering interest rates. Perhaps the British government is worried about inflation so it wants to cut the money supply by reducing bank borrowing. In this case it could raise the interest rate. A Canadian investor, spotting that interest rates are higher in London than Toronto, may then be tempted to change their Canadian dollars to pounds and deposit them in British banks. But he or she would also have to take into account differences in the rates of inflation. There is little point in moving funds into the UK for a few percentage points difference in the interest rates if the value of your funds, which are now in pounds, is rapidly eroded by inflation. Moving currencies around is a tricky business.

### Enter the speculators

Exchange rates are thus affected by the costs of goods in different countries and by interest and inflation rates – and by the pressures of supply and demand resulting from cross-border trade. But exchange rates fluctuate much more rapidly than these fundamental factors would warrant; the value of international currencies bought and sold is vastly greater than the value of international trade. This suggests that something else is at work, encouraging people to move money in and out of currencies on a daily basis. In fact, volatility in the currency markets is largely the result of speculation.

Currency traders try to make their decisions based on events in the real world. So they always wait eagerly for data on imports and exports because these can signal potential changes in currency values. If Indonesian exports fall and imports rise, then supply and demand is likely to push down the value of the Indonesian rupiah. But traders can also amplify these trends by their own actions. Any trader who starts selling rupiah on the basis of a rise in Indonesian food imports will depress the demand for rupiah still further. Much of the activity in the foreign-exchange markets is driven not just by real events but by expectations. All of this results in frenzied activity, especially in London, the location for around one-third of foreign exchange trading.

The costs of trading are low, as little as 0.01 per cent on each deal, and screen-based transactions are completed in milliseconds.[5] This allows traders to respond on the slightest whim, or the guess of a change in interest rates or inflation figures, shifting around millions of dollars at a time.

Foreign-exchange trading is also hugely profitable. In the US, for example, for the big commercial banks, foreign-exchange dealing accounts for a significant proportion of their profits. Banks, however, are not trading on their own account but on behalf of their customers. In some cases this gives them the opportunity to collude with other banks to offer clients a bad deal, effectively stealing money from them. In November 2014, six major banks were fined more than $4 billion for rigging foreign-exchange markets. The culprits were UBS, Citi, JPMorgan Chase, HSBC, Royal Bank of Scotland and Bank of America.[6]

## Exchange-rate systems

Nowadays, partly as a result of this intensive trading, honest and dishonest, the rates for most of the world's major currencies fluctuate daily – a far cry from the more sedate era when currencies scarcely moved since most of them were yoked together via the 'gold standard'. This standard emerged around the middle of the 19th century when the central banks of most Western countries behaved in a highly disciplined fashion, only issuing new paper currency that corresponded to the value of gold in their vaults. So in principle anyone with a banknote could exchange this for the value in gold at a fixed rate. The Bank of England embraced the gold standard in 1821, followed by Australia and Canada and later by Germany, Scandinavia, Holland, Belgium, Switzerland, France, Finland and the United States. Later the system spread to Asia, including Japan, the Straits Settlements, India and the Philippines. By 1910 most nations were on the gold standard.

At the beginning of the 20th century, for example, £1 was fixed at 22 ounces of gold, and $1 at 4.5 ounces. Divide one weight by the other and you get a fixed exchange rate in which £1 was worth $4.86 – with corresponding ratios between other currencies. This offered a way of settling imbalances between countries using flows of gold. If France, for example, successfully exported more wine to Germany, and accumulated deutschmarks, it could exchange these for gold with the Bundesbank. Imbalances were therefore resolved by transfers of gold into and out of countries.

The gold standard broke down temporarily from 1914 with the outbreak of the First World War. As a result of paying for troops and equipment, the warring countries soon exhausted their supplies of gold and suspended the promise to exchange banknotes for gold. For the losing country, Germany, this would eventually lead to the collapse of its currency. Faced with demands for reparations from the victors, the German government printed a large number of banknotes. Such was the pace of inflation that a single egg was eventually priced at four billion deutschmarks. The world record for hyperinflation, however, was established in this era by Hungary. The national currency, the pengo, was soon expressed in 'bilpengos', billions of pengos, and the central bank finally issued a 100 million bilpengo note that had to find room for 18 zeros.

After the First World War most countries returned to the gold standard. While this offered some stability, it did so at a heavy cost. Countries with imbalances that were losing gold would see their reserves dwindle. Smaller central bank reserves meant less money in the banking system. If people could not borrow, this would reduce demand so prices could fall – resulting in 'deflation'. At this point the economy would go into recession. To some extent the system was self-correcting: if consumers were unable to afford so many foreign goods, imports would fall below exports, and the flows of gold could be reversed. The foreign-exchange accounts would be wrenched back into balance. The economy might be stable again, but at a lower level, with many people unemployed.

After the Second World War a conference at Bretton Woods in New Hampshire, which also saw the establishment of the World Bank and the International Monetary Fund (IMF), introduced a somewhat more flexible system. This effectively meant that the US fixed the dollar to gold, at $35 per ounce, and other countries fixed their currencies to the dollar at a 'par' value. This 'Gold Exchange System' required central banks to buy and sell their currencies so as to keep them within one per cent of the 'par' value. This did not apply to ordinary citizens, however, who were no longer allowed to cash in their dollars for gold.[7]

This system was not as rigid as the gold standard since countries suffering persistent balance-of-payments problems could under certain circumstances either devalue their currencies to a lower exchange rate, or borrow gold or foreign exchange from the IMF to tide them over. Within this system, the British pound was steadily devalued, from $4.03 in 1944, to $2.80 in 1949, to $2.40 in 1967. In 1976 the British government was also to suffer the ignominy of going 'cap in hand' to the IMF for a loan of $2.3 billion.

Eventually the Bretton Woods exchange system also broke down, and for an all-too-familiar reason: war. The US came off this fixed standard in 1971 because financing the war in Vietnam was draining its gold reserves. Subsequently other developed countries decided that their countries could 'float' against the dollar, much as they do today. But floating does not suit all countries. Those with more fragile monetary systems decided not to risk instability. Instead they preferred to fix, or 'peg' their currency to another one, commonly the US dollar. So as the dollar went up and down in a more controlled fashion, their currency would follow suit. As an extension of this system, governments can also establish a 'currency board' – a new monetary authority which takes over one of the central bank's functions, that of issuing the national currency. A currency board can only issue new banknotes if it has received corresponding new supplies of foreign exchange.

The main problem with any fixed-rate system is that stability is achieved only at the price of a loss of government control over monetary policy. Governments and central banks value the flexibility offered by manipulating interest rates. They may want to increase interest rates to control inflation, for example, or reduce them if they are faced with high unemployment and want to stimulate economic activity. But if they have a fixed or pegged rate, then in order to keep the currency at this rate they have to adjust the interest rate – raising it to attract foreign capital, for example, if the exchange rate is under pressure. If governments use interest rates primarily to support the currency, they lose the freedom to adjust rates in accordance with the need to control inflation or encourage employment.

## Currency crises

There is a limit to which governments can defend their exchange rates. If the rates get too far out of line with a country's economic fundamentals then the illusionary security of fixed rates can be followed by an implosion. This happened in 1997 in the Asian financial crisis that started in Thailand. While the crisis had multiple causes in different countries, currency pegs played their part. In Thailand during the early 1990s, the currency – the baht – was pegged at 25 to the dollar. Meanwhile in the dollar's home, the United States, interest rates were very low. Thai companies and individuals took advantage of these low rates to borrow hefty sums in dollars, feeling confident that they would be able to earn enough baht to pay off their dollar debts by exchanging them at the bargain rate of 25 to the dollar. The result was millions of dollars' worth of speculative investment, particularly in flashy skyscrapers in Bangkok. All of this was also fostered by the Asian economic 'miracle', based on rapidly rising exports of electronic and other goods.

Then the deals started to unravel. First, the demand for Thailand's exports started to slow, putting pressure on the baht. Second, the US government became worried about inflation and so increased its interest rates – making it more difficult for Thai borrowers to service their loans. With the writing on the wall, speculators and investors started to lose faith that Thailand would defend the baht at 25 to the dollar and capital started to flee. This exacerbated the problem, eventually forcing the government to let the baht float, and in 1998 it duly soared to 56 to the dollar. People who had taken out dollar loans now had to earn more than twice as many baht to service them and many were forced into bankruptcy – leaving the Bangkok skyline in suspended animation, with half-finished buildings and idle cranes. The crisis then spread to other countries such as Indonesia, and even to stronger economies, including South Korea. But exchange-rate disasters do not happen only in developing countries. In 1992 the British government provided an iconic example of how not to control floating exchange rates – and lost over £3 billion in the process (see box).

Nevertheless, governments and central banks still try to manage exchange rates to some extent. They can do

---

### George Soros, the man who broke the Bank of England

In 1979, before the introduction of the euro, the European Community devised the 'Exchange Rate Mechanism'. The aim was to stabilize currencies by allowing them to float within a limited range or 'band'. When the currency moved outside the band, the central bank had to adjust interest rates or buy or sell its currency to bring the exchange rate back into line. The UK joined the Exchange Rate Mechanism in 1990 but set an ambitiously high rate. By 1992, the pound was slipping out of its band – forcing the British government to take ever more desperate measures, raising interest rates and buying pounds.

Currency speculators sniffed an impending disaster – and an opportunity. The arch speculator was George Soros, then heading a hedge fund, the Quantum Fund. He did not believe |that the British government could sustain its defense and started to bet against the pound by selling 'futures' – contracts |to provide sterling in three or six months. Anticipating devaluation, he bought £6 billion worth. The showdown came on 'Black Wednesday', 16 September 1992. The British Conservative government frantically raised the base interest rate first to 10 per cent then to 12 per cent and finally to an eye-watering 15 per cent. Finally, and after spending £3.2 billion in a vain effort to prop up the pound, the authorities threw in the towel and conceded to the speculators, letting the pound float free. When the pound suddenly sank, Soros could provide his promised pounds at a rate far cheaper than he had bought them, walking away with around $1 billion in profit, and an enduring reputation as the 'man who broke the Bank of England'. ■

---

this simply by giving hints about future inflation data or possible changes in interest rates, or by actual changes. Or they may buy or sell currencies. Ultimately, however, they cannot influence long-term fundamental rates, since even national currency reserves are dwarfed by the volumes traded daily in the currency markets.

## Monetary unions

For countries that trade extensively with each other, it would be much more convenient to avoid the hassle of fluctuating exchange rates by sharing a common currency. The United States could be considered a monetary union, since it uses a single currency across 50 very different states. In the past such unions have been imposed by force by colonial powers. But more recently countries have entered into unions voluntarily.

The most notable case is that of the European Union where one currency, the euro, is used by 18 states. The euro and its interest rate are controlled by an independent body based in Frankfurt, the European Central Bank (ECB). The 18 national central-bank governors go to Frankfurt twice a month to rubber-stamp decisions taken by the ECB's executive board. The main argument in favor of a monetary union is that it creates a more stable environment. Consumers can compare prices in different countries. Companies do not have to worry that changes in exchange rates will affect their profits. And governments, particularly of smaller countries, do not have to worry about currency speculators ganging up on them.

The main disadvantage is the 'one-size-fits-all' approach. What suits one country in a monetary union will not suit another. All countries go through economic cycles, with periods of higher growth and low unemployment, followed by periods of lower growth and higher unemployment. It is unlikely that these cycles will coincide across member countries – which means that at any time some will have the wrong monetary policies. A country with high unemployment, for example, might want to have lower interest rates to stimulate growth, while one with higher growth might want a higher interest rate to dampen down inflation. The US, as a monetary union between states, appears to have a similar problem, but in this case there can be some equalization since workers can easily move from a depressed state to a faster-growing one. In principle, Europeans have the same flexibility, but in practice, despite scare stories about mass migration, workers are much more reluctant to relocate.

Before entering the eurozone, countries were supposed to harmonize their economies and maintain low levels of budget deficits and inflation. In practice, few countries, not even France or Germany, kept to this bargain. This did not seem to matter when most economies were growing rapidly. As a result, they gained very easy access to credit with very few constraints. But the fundamental flaws in the eurozone were revealed following the global crisis in 2008. Several countries ran huge budget deficits and were finding it difficult to finance these by selling Eurobonds. In 2010 and 2011, Greece, Ireland and Portugal had to be bailed out – by the IMF and the European Union – under conditions of severe austerity. This proved unpopular in the recipient countries, as government workers lost their jobs, as well as in richer countries, whose citizens found themselves subsidizing welfare systems seemingly more generous than their own. After a couple of years the bailouts appeared to have stabilized their economies, if at huge social cost.

But by late 2014 the situation was starting to deteriorate again and in early 2015 the ECB had to intervene with a plan to create enough new euros to buy €60 billion a month of mainly public-sector Eurobonds issued by a range of eurozone countries.

This 'quantitative easing' was supposed to provide the bond's previous owners with the funds that they could lend elsewhere – though whether this will happen or not is another matter. However, the ECB said it would not buy Greek bonds unless the government maintained its austerity program.

The eurozone is by no means the only monetary union. A number of African countries, mostly former French colonies, have unions in West Africa and Central Africa that share a 'CFA franc', while others in the Pacific share a 'CFP franc'. In the Caribbean a group of smaller islands share the East Caribbean dollar.

## Dollarization

In modern monetary unions, countries enter into voluntary agreements through which they share the responsibility for monetary management. Some countries, however, have submitted to much more one-sided arrangements – abandoning their own currency and simply adopting that of a more powerful economy. Panama, for example, has long lived under the shadow of the United States. Although independent since 1903, it only gained control over its most valuable asset, the Canal, in 1999. Officially it has its own currency, the balboa, but issues this only in coins, and for most purposes uses the US dollar. US colonization also resulted in a legacy use of the dollar in other now independent states such as the Federated States of Micronesia.

Dollarization often happens unofficially during warfare or at a time of economic crisis that causes people to lose confidence in their own currency. When Timor-Leste, for example, gained its independence in 1999, it wanted to get rid of the Indonesian rupiah as soon as possible, and so adopted the US dollar. Although it now issues its own coins, centavos, which are equivalent to US cents, Timor-Leste still uses dollar bills.

Other countries have also collapsed into the dollar's embrace. In 2001 El Salvador established a dual currency system, using both the colón and the dollar, which were fixed at the same value. In practice, for nearly all commercial transactions people use dollars. The most contentious case, however, was in Ecuador. In 1999, Ecuador was in dire economic straits and had to default on government bonds. The following year, the President proposed to replace the national currency, the sucre, with the dollar. This outraged trade unions and indigenous population groups, who marched in protest. The army stepped in and replaced the President but his successor pressed on with dollarization anyway.

Countries that want to adopt another country's currency do not have to use the dollar. A number of European microstates, such as Montenegro, use the euro. The Vatican too uses the euro, though it is also allowed to produce a limited number of its own euro coins. In the Pacific, some of the small island states use the currencies of larger neighbours. The Cook Islands, for example, uses the New Zealand dollar and Kiribati and Nauru use the Australian dollar.

Why would any state want to give up the right to control its own currency? In some cases, it is because politicians have little faith in the monetary authorities, and fear that future governments that want to get out of an economic hole will be tempted to print money and thus trigger hyperinflation. Dollarization eliminates this risk and offers comfort to international investors, who will always know the dollar value of their investments. Dollarization also protects the country from attacks by currency speculators and helps exporters engage more easily in international trade.

But there are heavy costs. One is the loss of 'seigniorage'. This refers to the income that the government gains when it manufactures coins and notes that have a much higher value than their production cost, enabling it to spend or invest the difference. But the most serious disadvantage is a mirror image of one of the advantages. The government has fewer opportunities to make bad decisions but is also less able to make good ones – such as adjusting interest rates to boost employment. The central bank also has less freedom to support banks that get into difficulties. It might be able to lend some of its dollars, but without the flexibility to print money it cannot serve as the 'lender of last resort'. In 2014 the President of Ecuador was chafing at the bit, arguing that dollarization had reduced his capacity to manage the economy – that it was like 'boxing with one arm'.[8]

## Foreign-exchange reserves

Though few countries have resorted to dollarization, all will want to keep substantial quantities of dollars or other foreign currencies. Central banks have to hold reserves of foreign currency to act as a buffer in case of temporary trade or other deficits. In the case of dollars, for example, some of this is in dollar bills, but most will be in the form of US Treasury bonds or deposits in US banks.

Central banks can use these reserves to buy their own national currency if they want to push up the exchange rate so as to make imports cheaper. Globally, foreign-exchange reserves have been rising steeply. At the end of 2014, the reserves held by all countries came to $12 trillion. Of the reserves whose currency is known, around 60 per cent were held in US dollars and most of the rest in euros. In the past, the pound sterling was one of the world's major reserve currencies but now accounts for only around four per cent.[9]

In 2014 central banks outside the US were holding around $4 trillion. They can build up these reserves by hanging on to the dollars they have acquired by trading with the United States, or by buying foreign currency in the foreign-exchange markets. When other countries hoard dollars, this is effectively a huge gift to the United States. It is as though the US Treasury has been able to write $4 trillion in checks that no-one has ever cashed. Since 1975, this has enabled the US to embark on a long consumer boom and run a persistent annual trade deficit – $476 billion in 2013.[10] This all adds up. Divide $4 trillion by the US population and you find that each citizen on average now owes the rest of the world around $13,000. And this only corresponds to dollars held by foreign governments; even more US Treasury bonds are held by foreign corporations and individuals.

A number of countries have been able to boost their reserves substantially in recent years. Oil and gas exporters, including Russia, have benefited at times from periods of booming commodity prices. But the most striking increases have been in Asia. Some of this has come from success in manufactured exports. China, for example, by 2014 had accumulated $3.9 trillion in official reserves, of which $1.2 trillion was in US Treasury bonds.[11] But official reserves were also high in Japan at $1.2 trillion, and the Republic of Korea at $354 billion.[12]

This shift of reserves to Asia is one of the most remarkable transfers of global wealth in history. Following the 1997 financial crisis, Asian countries were understandably keen to avoid any repeat of that disaster and resolutely accumulated reserves as a kind of insurance policy. They could do this because the industrialized countries were investing in Asia to take advantage of low labor costs and the prospect of new markets. Asian countries responded by selling manufactured goods to the West. Rather than spending this, however, they recycled a significant part of the proceeds into US Treasury and government bonds.

As a result, they now have vast sums far beyond what they need for safety. You might think this is dangerous. What happens if China starts to sell some of its dollar

| *Official reserves assets, 2014, US dollars, millions* | | |
|---|---|---|
| 1 | Japan | 1,269,079 |
| 2 | Saudi Arabia | 740,400 |
| 3 | Euro Area | 739,479 |
| 4 | Switzerland | 526,172 |
| 5 | Russian Federation | 418,880 |
| 6 | Brazil | 375,426 |
| 7 | Korea, Republic of | 363,095 |
| 8 | China, P.R.: Hong Kong | 327,930 |
| 9 | India | 315,558 |
| 10 | Singapore | 260,553 |
| 11 | Mexico | 196,719 |
| 12 | Germany | 194,016 |
| 13 | Thailand | 158,544 |
| 14 | France | 141,944 |
| 15 | Italy | 141,609 |
| 16 | United Kingdom | 39,476 |
| 17 | United States | 134,571 |
| 18 | Turkey | 133,452 |
| 19 | Malaysia | 125,731 |
| 20 | Indonesia | 111,144 |
| 21 | Poland | 100,394 |
| 22 | Israel | 86,314 |

Source: data.imf.org

bonds? A lower demand for dollars would cause the dollar to fall – and import prices to rise. No more cheap TVs or smartphones. But the Asian countries would need to think twice before dumping their dollars. If international markets believed that China was going to sell its dollars, the dollar would nosedive – reducing the value of Asia's hard-earned assets. This is rather like the relationship between a bank and its customers. If you borrow a small amount from the bank, the bank owns you. If you borrow a huge amount, then you 'own' the bank, which will be terrified that you will default.

Nevertheless, many people in Asia are becoming restless about the use of their funds to prop up the US economy and have suggested better uses for the money. One possibility is investing in infrastructure. Across Asia, roads, railways, energy plants, airports, sea ports, telecommunications grids and bridges are creaking under the strain of economic growth. In late 2014, China, for example, announced it would contribute $40 billion to a new Silk Road infrastructure fund to build roads, railways, ports and airports linking China with Central Asia and South Asia.[13]

Unfortunately, while Asia was learning the lessons of its financial crisis and was squirrelling its savings around the world, other countries had embarked on reckless financial adventures that were to bring the global economy to its knees. The causes and consequences of the ensuing 2008 financial crisis are the subject of the next chapter.

**1** C Eagleton and J Williams, *Money: a history,* British Museum Press, London, 2007. **2** Dagfinn Rime and Andreas Schrimp, 'The anatomy of the global FX market through the lens of the 2013 Triennial Survey', in *BIS Quarterly Review,* December 2013. **3** World Trade Organization, *Latest Quarterly Trade Trends,* Geneva, 2014, nin.tl/wtotradetrends **4** economics.com/content/big-mac-index **5** *Financial Centres,* Economist Intelligence Unit, London, 2008. **6** Daniel Schäfer, Caroline Binham, and Kara Scannell, 'Regulators slap $4.3bn fines on six banks in global forex probe', *Financial Times,* 12 November 2014. **7** David Graeber, *Debt: the First 5,000 years,* Melvyn House, London, 2012. **8** Nathan Gill, 'Ecuador's Dollarization Architect Doubts Correa's Pledge', *Bloomberg,* nin.tl/ecuadordoubts **9** Currency Composition of Official Foreign Exchange Reserves (COFER), IMF, 2014, imf.org/external/np/sta/cofer/eng/index.htm **10** 'International Economic Accounts', US Department of Commerce, 2014 bea.gov/international/index.htm **11** James Kynge and Josh Noble, 'China: Turning away from the dollar', *Financial Times,* 9 December 2014. **12** Data Template on International Reserves and Foreign Currency Liquidity, IMF, 2014, nin.tl/liquiditytable **13** 'China to establish $40 billion Silk Road infrastructure fund', Reuters, 2014, nin.tl/silkroadfund

# 6 The 2008 crash: debt-driven disaster

In the 2000s banks created huge amounts of money to lend to hopeful homeowners. But these debts were resting on very fragile foundations. When these collapsed, the results were spectacular. Banks failed, governments panicked and anxious savers wondered whether their funds were about to disappear. The situation may appear to have stabilized but this is an illusion. The underlying flaws remain and debt is starting to rise again.

INTERNATIONAL CAPITALISM, AND particularly finance, is inherently unstable. If you believed classical economic theory you might dispute this. In theory, efficient markets, left to their own devices, will reach a state of equilibrium where demand is forever balanced by supply – whether of goods or services or money. In the case of money, however, this is never true. A system based on credit, which literally means 'belief', will, like any human institution, be prone to rapid shifts in sentiment, from long waves of optimism to sudden crises of confidence.[1]

These crises have become increasingly frequent. One study found that in the period 1949 to 1971 there were 48 financial crises around the world, but that in the period 1973 to 1997 there were 139.[2] They have also become increasingly serious: the way that financial markets have developed in recent years has amplified the normal mood swings of economic cycles into full-blown manic depression.

The global collapse from 2008 had multiple origins. It had links, for example, with the Asian financial crisis of the late 1990s which taught many Asian countries that at all costs they should avoid the problems that would drive them to borrow from the IMF and be subjected to conditions that undermined their economies and further impoverished their people. Instead they would build up their own insurance by saving huge sums, some of which could be parked in the United States.

This may have seemed prudent, but indirectly it boosted the availability of credit in the US, presenting ready sources of easy loans that people could use to buy houses they could not really afford. Regulations, or the lack of them, also played their part. The Basel rules, for example, had the perverse effect of encouraging banks to devise ever more dangerous loopholes. On the other hand, the repeal in 1999 of the Glass-Steagall Act in the US tempted more banks into high-risk investment banking. The crisis also had technological origins, notably in the availability of cheap computer power, which allowed financial wizards to conjure up astonishing piles of interlinked derivatives balanced precariously on the same shaky underlying assets.

## Bubble after bubble

A convenient starting point for the story is the year 2000. The stock markets were just recovering from a technological crash – the dotcom bubble that started in 1995 and was based on the blind faith that any company doing anything on the shiny new internet would make vast sums of money. Surely, it was thought, the normal rules no longer applied and any dotcom enterprise, from pets.com to smells.com, would grab enough global market share that its value would soar into the stratosphere forever.

Stock values certainly rose rapidly. The US stock exchange on which most dotcom stocks were traded, the NASDAQ, increased fivefold from 1995, when the internet browser Netscape was launched, to reach a giddy peak in March 2000. Then the bubble burst. Eighteen months later the NASDAQ was back where it started – wiping out $4.4 trillion in share prices, at that time the largest stock-market collapse in the history of industrial capitalism.[3]

The essential characteristic of that bubble, like many others, was the assumption that the value of something, from stocks to houses, will rise forever. Even if you know this is nonsense, you can still make money on the way up, providing you get off the escalator before it tips you over a cliff. The problem, and thus the opportunity, is that no-one knows exactly when to step off.

Moreover, the dotcom bubble was also to sow the seeds of the 'sub-prime' disaster. Following the stock-market crash, the US Federal Reserve, anxious to get the economy moving again, rapidly pushed down interest rates, from 6.5 to 3.5 per cent. No sooner had Wall Street absorbed that information than al-Qaeda appeared in the skies on 11 September, 2001. In response, the Fed lowered interest rates still further. By 2003, they were down to one per cent.

### Here we go again

For several years US interest rates were below the rate of inflation – so real interest rates were negative. In these circumstances the sensible thing to do was to borrow as much as you could to buy something that would rise in value while the low cost of your loan was eroded by inflation. And what safer option could there be than buying your own home?

For most people, buying a house is their largest-ever personal transaction. It is also the one most likely to be achieved with borrowed funds. Even the most prudent households do not blink at taking on a huge loan to buy a house, since the mortgage repayments appear similar to rent, with the crucial advantage that after 20 or 30 years you will finish up owning your home. House purchase is thus, in financial terms, a highly 'leveraged' but apparently safe transaction.

Like any other leveraged activity, however, the

viability of house purchasing is acutely sensitive to changes in interest rates. As interest rates stayed low, not just in the US but in many other countries, people were more attracted by the prospect of buying their own house or even a second or third one to rent out. In response, house prices in many countries, particularly the US, the UK, Spain and France, shot up.

Worryingly, the pattern is now being repeated. In order to stimulate their economies, central banks have again pushed down interest rates – often close to zero. Why save money in the bank where it will lose value? Better to invest in property. Predictably, house prices are

## (Un)safe as houses

Before the financial crisis in 2008, low interest rates fuelled a house-price boom around the world. The graph illustrates how this played out in the UK and shows average house prices, adjusted for inflation, over the period 1976 to 2014. In today's pounds, a house that in 1976 was worth £78,000, by 2008 was worth £217,000. Prices fell after the crash but in recent years have been rising again.

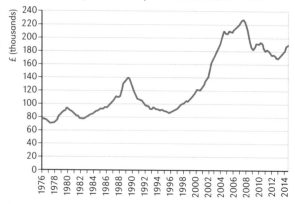

*Inflation-adjusted house prices in the UK, 1976-2014*

Source: *Nationwide house price index*, Nationwide, 2014,
nin.tl/housepricesUK

rising around the world. Particularly worrying at present are the prices in Canada and New Zealand where, taking into account the national levels of incomes and rents, houses on average are considered to be overvalued by around 25 per cent.[4]

The effect of housing bubbles will depend to some extent on the nature of the mortgages. In the UK, the bank or building society will probably take as security the deeds of the property. Nevertheless, the borrower remains liable for the full amount of the loan. This is called a 'recourse loan'. The 1980s UK housing boom was followed by a sudden collapse which left many people paying mortgages for properties that had lost value – they were in 'negative equity'. When the monthly interest charges became unpayable, they could not simply sell the house to pay off the loan since the sale value would no longer cover the loan. This was enough to force many households into bankruptcy.

Another serious implication of a house-price boom is that it dramatically increases inequality. If you are lucky enough to own a house at the beginning of the boom then you will make a huge unearned profit if you choose to sell. But if you are a first-time buyer, then things are much more difficult, since, even if interest rates are low, you will find it hard to borrow enough to get on the housing ladder.

## Crazy loans

When house prices are rising faster than incomes, then a shortage of cash should cool things down. If there are no new credit-worthy buyers then prices should stabilize. Unfortunately, in the 2000s financiers in the US managed to devise a system through which, despite soaring house prices, many of the poorest people were still able to buy. This involved a series of intermediaries who effectively shielded lenders from the borrowers. Previously, when a bank manager lent funds to buy a house, he or she would interview the borrower to make sure they could repay. But from around 2000 the people in the US who were providing the funds had very little idea of whom they were lending to, and how risky the loans were.

Instead, the loans were arranged by mortgage brokers who signed up new borrowers, working on commission. By 2003, they were running out of potential new house owners since, based on sensible terms, no-one could afford to buy. The brokers thus had to devise ever more seductive arrangements to ensnare people who were poor credit risks – the 'sub-prime' borrowers. For example, they would ask for little or no down payment and start out charging very low interest rates, while having a very high rate kick in later – a 'balloon mortgage'. And, rather than asking for evidence of income, they would take borrowers at their word – 'self-certification'. The results were often 'ninja' loans – to people with 'no income, no job, no assets'.

Borrowers went along with this, either because they had no idea of what they were committing themselves to, or because they reasoned that with house prices rising they would later be able to sell at a profit. This seemed like a one-way bet. A further encouragement was that, in some cases, mortgages in the US, particularly in California, can be 'non-recourse' loans, which means that ultimately the borrower can just send the bank the keys to the house ('jingle mail'), leaving the bank with no further claim. The outcome of all this was that a steadily increasing proportion of loans were going to sub-prime borrowers who were likely to default. Between 2001 and 2005, the total value of sub-prime loans rose from 5 per cent of the total to around 20 per cent.[5]

### Insecure securitization

You can see why the borrowers and the brokers might collude in this ever slacker lending system. But what of the banks? They, after all, are regulated and there are limits to the loans they can make. According to the Basel agreements, for every loan they add to their balance sheets, they need to have sufficient capital to serve as a buffer against borrowers defaulting. Unfortunately, while the Basel rules promised to make banks seem safer, they had the perverse effect of encouraging the financial wizards to find ways around the rules – to evade the capital requirement by pushing the loans off banks' balance sheets.

Here the key was 'securitization' – converting mortgage repayments into securities that acted like bonds. As an illustrative aside, it is worth noting that anything that produces a fairly predictable flow of income can be sold as a security. One of the most notable was in 1997 when David Bowie sold $55 million-worth of 'Bowie Bonds', which entitled the buyers to a share in the revenue from his first 25 albums over a period of 10 years.[6] Unfortunately Bowie's earnings did not prove as high as expected and by 2004 Moody's Investor Service was rating these bonds, all of which had been bought by the Prudential Insurance Co of America, at a little above junk status.

Mortgages too should produce a steady stream of income. But since converting only one or two mortgages into a bond would produce a security too dependent on repayments by individual borrowers, a bank can instead spread the risk by collecting a large number of mortgages together into a single package that can be sold as a bundle of new securities with the clumsy name of 'collateralized debt obligations' (CDOs).

For the investors, the advantage was that they could become players in the domestic mortgage market without the messy business of selling loans or collecting arrears from real people. If they wanted to know how much these products were worth, they could just ask the ratings agencies. By 2003, agencies such as Moody's or

Fitch derived 40 to 50 per cent of their income from this kind of structured finance.[7] Unfortunately, since they were in no position to fully assess these highly complex products themselves, the ratings agencies relied for information on the issuers of CDOs.

The effect of all this was to further distance the borrower from the lender. Everybody along the chain was happy. The borrowers were offered loans to buy houses. The mortgage brokers picked up their commissions on each sale. The banks collected fees for setting up and servicing the loan contracts. The investors benefited from a range of juicy-looking securities.

Structured mortgage finance took off in a big way. And the structures became ever more arcane. All sorts of elaborations entered the mix. Not just combinations of fixed- and floating-rate mortgages, but other types of derivatives, such as credit default swaps. The securities houses were also churning out more conventional CDOs based on other assets that could deliver a regular income, such as credit-card loans, or commercial property. But by 2006 most of the CDOs were being issued for domestic property loans, of which around two-thirds were sub-prime. Previously, the securities dealers would have had to run their mainframes for several days to compute who was entitled to what. But the rapid development of personal computers and workstations was now making light work of these calculations.

## The bubble bursts

But what did this all mean? Ultimately the only people who knew what went into the CDOs were the geeks who devised them and even they were unable to predict the outcome of all possible scenarios. Meanwhile, the directors of banks, insurance companies and pension schemes saw only the glossy prospectuses illustrating securities that would offer higher yields than other comparably rated corporate bonds. The problem was, of course, that all these superimposed computerized constructions were resting on flimsy foundations.[8]

You might wonder what the US government was doing. After all, a central bank is supposed to worry about inflation and the rising prices of houses and to raise interest rates accordingly. But overall inflation in the US had remained persistently low. This was partly because Asian countries were still supplying vast amounts of consumer goods. This kept US prices down. Asian central banks invested much of the proceeds into US government bonds. This kept the dollar high, which further depressed the cost of imports for US consumers.

The US government might also have worried about the price of housing. But, rather than trying to deflate the bubble in house prices, the then chair of the Federal Reserve, Alan Greenspan, encouraged people to take out home loans. The conventional view was that there was no such thing as a bubble – or at least no way to distinguish a bubble from an underlying rise in the price of property. Out in the real world, the mortgage brokers could have told Greenspan something different. They were running out of people to whom they could legitimately sell new loans and so were making increasingly perilous offers. The danger was not immediately evident because while the market was rising the defaults, even for sub-prime loans, were quite small. But once the brokers finally pushed buyers over the edge, the defaults started to rise.

The bubble had to burst, and in 2007 it duly did. The first sequence of pops emerged from the hedge funds. They had bought enormous quantities of those high-yielding sub-prime CDOs. But in their usual style they had done so with borrowed money. When the ratings of CDOs suddenly started to slip they were in trouble, and since they held huge quantities of bonds even small drops in value were leveraged or magnified into huge potential losses.

Another characteristic of these derivative markets is that they often involve private 'over-the-counter' deals. CDOs are not traded on exchanges. This means that there is no public record of who owns what. And no-one is ever sure of the market price. Moreover, with no exchange, there may be no ready buyer. Among the first to panic was the investment bank Bear Stearns, which owned a couple of hedge funds and was saddled with near worthless CDOs. Suddenly it started selling anything it could. As there was no market for the CDOs, it had to dispose of everything else. Thus a crisis that started in the housing market was suddenly infecting other areas of a complex, interlinked financial system.

This contagious crisis then hit the banks. They thought they had securitized thousands of mortgages off their balance sheets. But not quite. In some cases this was because when some banks issued the CDOs they had also offered guarantees against heavy defaults occurring soon after issue. As the defaults rose the buyers duly claimed their money back and the toxic sludge oozed back onto the banks' balance sheets. But there were also other entanglements. Banks might, for example, have used credit default swaps to insure their corporate bonds, only to discover that the institutions that had provided the insurance had also taken loans from them.[9] Oh dear.

Worse still, many of these banks had been taking risks that most people would have regarded as reckless beyond belief. Banks are supposed to retain sufficient capital to bolster themselves against the prospect that some loans will not be repaid. But keeping cash lying idle is expensive, so many of them had not bothered. In 2007, the largest banks in the US and the UK (Citi and the Royal Bank of Scotland) for every $100 in loans were capable of absorbing only $2 of losses. No wonder they crashed.[10]

## Crunch time

Now we are at the credit crunch. The banks are running scared. No-one really knows who owes what to whom. Suddenly nobody trusts anybody for fear that they will go bust. The usual process of lending between banks seizes up. The 'money markets', consisting of banks and other big institutions, desperately hang on to what they have got. And if they do lend at all they charge cripplingly high interest rates. If you have plenty of cash, you can sit tight. If not, even if you are solvent you may be in trouble.

Enter the British bank Northern Rock. Ironically, Northern Rock was brought to its knees not by risky lending but by risky borrowing. The former building society was lending much of its money to commercial landlords or to individuals who were buying property to let. Since it did not have enough people saving money in its branches to provide the necessary reserves, it had to look elsewhere. The strategy was to base 25 per cent of its lending on savers' deposits, 50 per cent on securitization, and 25 per cent on borrowing from the money markets.[11] What the clever managers of Northern Rock never bargained for was that the money markets would seize up – and refuse to roll over their loans on any terms. In September 2008 it had to ask the Bank of England for help. Savers heard the news and took fright, though, being British, the 'run on the bank' took the form of orderly queues. The British government dithered, then made loans to tide the bank over, but six months later had to nationalize it to keep it afloat.

Elsewhere too the dominoes were starting to topple. In 2007 the giant Swiss bank UBS said it had lost $37 billion in sub-prime investments. In March 2008 Bear Stearns, which a year earlier had been valued at around $40 billion, was bought by JPMorgan Chase for just $240 million. In the UK, the Royal Bank of Scotland soon found itself running short of capital.

## Meltdown

By mid-2008, the threat of total financial meltdown had spurred governments into dramatic action. At first they tried to prop up the banks by extending credit. The US Federal Reserve came up with a $700-billion package. But this was not enough. Many banks were becoming not just illiquid (short of immediate funds) but insolvent (with more debts than assets). They needed more assets to serve as capital, and so would have to issue more shares. At that point the only feasible buyers of shares were governments – so the effect would be partial or complete nationalization. In September 2008 the US government took over the country's two giant housing corporations, the Federal National Mortgage Association, nicknamed Fannie Mae, and the Federal Home Mortgage Corporation, Freddie Mac.

In the UK, the government then nationalized the Bradford and Bingley bank and in October announced that, in order to boost bank capital, it was buying stakes in many other banks, including LloydsTSB, the Royal Bank of Scotland and HBOS – to the tune of around £37 billion. Taxpayers would own 60 per cent of the Royal Bank of Scotland and 40 per cent of the merged LloydsTSB and HBOS.

Meanwhile, in the US, the government had declined to rescue the country's fourth-largest investment bank, Lehman Brothers. This duly went bust, with huge repercussions for its counterpart banks around the world. The largest investment bank, Merrill Lynch, was taken over by Bank of America. Eventually, with other banks in peril, the Treasury Secretary followed the British lead and in October announced that the government would spend $250 billion on part-nationalizing a number of American banks and the main insurance company AIG. Socialism had come to America.

It should be noted, however, that banks had not been so reckless everywhere. In Canada, for example, no banks were bailed out. None were in danger of failing, then or now. The World Economic Forum produces a ranking on the soundness of banking sectors. In 2014-15, the top three rankings were taken by Canada, New Zealand and Australia. The United States was ranked 49 and the UK was ranked 89.[12]

## The rest of the world takes a hit

The drama had started in the US and the UK, the world's leading financial centers, but other countries soon felt the pain. This was because transnational banks and other institutions became desperate for cash. Since they could not sell their 'toxic' assets, they had to sell a lot of their healthy ones instead, which included shares in companies in developing countries. They rushed into 'fire sales' of the securities they held, thus depressing their prices, and consequently cut the value of the portfolios of other banks that held similar securities.

When the banks stopped lending, the effect was a global 'credit crunch'. Companies could not access funds to finance their activities – for example, to buy stock in advance of sales. This crippled the global economy. Previously world output had been increasing by around 2.2 per cent a year. But in 2009 it fell by 1.8 per cent – the biggest decline since World War Two.[13] The immediate impact was a global loss of around 20 million jobs – half of which were in manufacturing. But that was just the start. The job losses persisted year after year. The ILO estimated that in 2014 the world still had 62 million fewer jobs than it would have had without the crisis. Even this seriously underestimated the damage, since it corresponded only to the jobs lost in developed countries. In poorer countries, where people have little prospect of unemployment benefits, the impact is disguised as underemployment or lower wages.[14]

## Crisis response

Governments struggled to cope with the consequences. As well as bailing out errant banks, they now had to deal with a collapse in their 'real economies'. To try to get things going, they wanted people to borrow and spend more so they cut interest rates. In the UK and the US, for example, in 2009 the central banks cut interest rates to virtually zero – 0.25 per cent. In normal circumstances, this should encourage people to borrow money cheaply and spend it. Governments also tried to encourage household spending by cutting taxes.

In addition, they tried to put more money in people's pockets by increasing public spending. Building a new bridge, for example, would not just put money in the bank accounts of engineers and construction workers, but this would subsequently pass into the accounts of shopkeepers when they spent this money and then ripple in a 'multiplier' effect through the rest of the economy.

The sums of money involved in these government stimulus packages were huge. In the US, the $785-billion package announced in 2009 amounted to four per cent of the country's GDP.

Something similar happened in Asia. Many countries had been hard hit by the sudden drop in demand for garments and electronic gadgets. Governments here also responded with stimulus packages. In late 2008, China spent $584 billion, equivalent to around 13 per cent of GDP, largely on infrastructure. The government of South Korea introduced a package equivalent to around four per cent of GDP.[15] Similar programs were introduced in Thailand, Malaysia and Singapore.

When reducing interest rates and increasing public spending did not seem to be doing the trick, some governments resorted to creating more money – by typing larger numbers into the accounts of the central bank. The aim was to increase the quantity of money in circulation, so this is called 'quantitative easing' (QE). To inject this into the economy, they could have printed it and then dropped it from the sky as 'helicopter money'. Or, in a more sophisticated form, they could have added, a suitable bonus to everyone's bank account. Instead they used it to buy back long-term government bonds from financial institutions at attractive prices. In theory this should give the banks and other institutions more money that they can lend out at lower interest rates. By December 2014 the Bank of England had bought back £375 billion worth of such bonds.[16]

One of the initial worries was that QE would stoke long-term inflation. This has not yet happened since inflation in the UK by early 2015 had fallen to around one per cent. Ultimately of greater concern is the way the money has been used. Much of it resurfaced for speculation in property, shares and commodities. Handing out cheques to everyone would have seen it used more productively. And, while QE does seem to have helped maintain spending, many of the positive benefits were subsequently offset by harsh austerity programs that took money out of people's pockets.[17]

## Deeper in debt

These stimulus packages affected government finances and added to public debt. But what hit government revenues hardest in this period was actually their lower revenues. As individuals and companies saw their incomes fall, they spent less, and paid less in taxes. For richer governments this should not be a matter of much concern, since the swing of the economic cycle will see their economies recover, and along with it their tax revenues. Moreover, if they manage their own currency they can ultimately just print more money and inflate their way out of debt – though this will cause pain in terms of more expensive imports.

If they do not manage their own currencies they are in more serious trouble. This is effectively what happened to a number of European countries, notably Greece, Ireland, Portugal and Spain. They, along with seven other countries, use a common currency, the euro, which is managed by the European Central Bank. An underlying premise of any common currency area is that all members will 'harmonize' their economic activities so that they can all use one currency of the same value. Given the economic, political and cultural diversity among member countries, this was always a heroic assumption. In fact it enabled some of the weaker countries to borrow large sums by issuing bonds in euros at low interest rates. The bond buyers assumed that the bonds were safe, because the euro also had the backing of sturdier economies such as those of Germany and the Netherlands. There could thus be no question of default.

After the financial crisis, however, the flaws in the euro appeared and bond buyers got cold feet. Ireland had to bail out its banks and was faced with huge budget deficits. Greece was already overspending, with notoriously generous pension systems. When it was time for these governments to roll over their debts by issuing new bonds, they found this more difficult and expensive. Now there was a real prospect of default. If they had still been using Irish punts or Greek drachmae, there would have been an automatic correction through a fall in the exchange rate. This would have been painful since it would have made salaries indirectly worth less in terms of imported goods. But, as a member of the euro, whose value is largely set by richer economies, this could not happen. Instead the only way of balancing budgets sufficiently to reassure the bond markets seemed to be an 'internal devaluation' – cutting salaries and generally slashing public expenditure.

By the beginning of 2015, the global financial and economic picture appeared to have stabilized – but at a huge financial and human cost. Governments in the main financial centers had announced measures to control the banks so as to try to stop this happening again. But the chances are that the drama will play out again. In a money-driven economy, the story arc – from boom to bust and back again – will inevitably recur. There must be better ways to create and control money. And that is the subject of the final chapter.

**1** G Cooper, *The Origin of Financial Crises: Central Banks, credit bubbles and the efficient market fallacy*, Harriman House, Petersfield, 2008. **2** M Bordo and B Eichengreen, *Crisis Now and Then: What Lessons from the Last Era of Financial Globalization*, National Bureau of Economic Research, Working Paper 8716, Cambridge, Mass, 2002. **3** B Goldfarb, D Kirsch and D Miller, *Was there too little entry during the Dot Com Era?* Robert H Smith School of Business, University of Maryland, Working Paper no RHS-06-029, ssrn.com/abstract=899100 **4** 'Global property markets: Frothy again', *The Economist*, 20 August 2014. **5** C Morris, *The Trillion Dollar Meltdown*, Public Affairs, New York, 2008. **6** 'Bankers Hope for a Reprise Of "Bowie Bonds"', *The Wall Street Journal*, 23 August 2005. **7** *The role of ratings in structured finance: issues and implications*, Committee on the Global Financial System, Bank for International Settlements, Basel, 2005. **8** Morris, op cit, p 78. **9** 'Prime movers', *The Economist*, 9 April 2007. **10** 'Making banks safe: Calling to accounts', *The Economist*, 5 October 2013. **11** B Walters, *The fall of Northern Rock*, Harriman House, Petersfield, 2008. **12** *Global Competitiveness Report 2014-15*, World Economic Forum, Geneva, 2014. **13** Stijn Claessens, M. Ayhan Kose, Luc Laeven & Fabián Valencia, *Understanding Financial Crises: Causes, Consequences, and Policy Responses*, IMF, Washington, 2014. **14** *Global Employment Trends 2014: Risk of a jobless recovery?*, ILO, Geneva, 2014. **15** *Economic and Social Survey of Asia and the Pacific 2009*, UNESCAP, Bangkok, 2009. **16** Bank of England, 2014, bankofengland. co.uk accessed 20 December 2014. **17** Larry Elliott, 'Quantitative easing: giving cash to the public would have been more effective', *The Guardian*, 29 October 2014.

# 7 How to get our money back

**Money is too important to be left to bankers, whose greed and incompetence have resulted in a financial system capable of giving them grotesque incomes but exposing everyone else to endless cycles of risk and crisis. Time for a radical change.**

FINANCIAL SERVICES ARE now one of the largest economic sectors and are taking more of our money. One of the most extreme cases is the UK, where the banking sector's assets, at around £5 trillion, are already equivalent to four times the country's total annual output. Worryingly, the Bank of England estimates that by 2050 banking will grow to £60 trillion – more than nine times national output.[1] In the US the scale of banking is disguised somewhat because many banks have securitized their assets off their balance sheets. But taking this into account it has been estimated that total banking assets are around 170 per cent of US GDP.[2]

The financial-services industry justifies this frenzied activity on the grounds that it meets with exquisite precision the needs of borrowers and investors, as financial markets respond to subtle shifts in supply and demand. In reality, it has become a mechanism for transferring wealth into the pockets of a financial élite. This is termed the 'croupier's take' – the amount skimmed off by financial intermediaries such as the investment banks, brokers, traders and the operators of mutual funds. This has produced huge profits. In the 1960s financial-sector firms accounted for only 1 per cent of UK profits; by 2010, they accounted for 15 per cent.[3]

How do we break out of this dismal cycle? How do we get our money back? The starting point is to recognize that money is not a fixed or absolute object like a gold ingot or a silver dollar. Rather it is just information – a way of quantifying relationships between buyers and sellers, borrowers and lenders.

Throughout our lives we build up a complex set of obligations – between siblings, neighbors and friends, governments and citizens, employers and employees, businesses and customers. Some of these relationships are quantified in cash terms, but most are not, particularly those within families. Family financial relationships are often huge, especially those between parents and children. In the UK, for example, it has been estimated that raising a child to age 21 costs on average £227,266.[4] In the US, the average figure for raising a child to age 17 can be up to $506,610.[5] Fortunately for the reproduction of the human species, few parents keep accurate accounts, and fewer still will present their children with a nasty bill on their 21st birthday. On the contrary, nowadays the 'bank of mum and dad' often continues to subsidize children well into adulthood. In 2014, UK parents shelled out on average £400 ($640) per 18 to 25-year-old son or daughter.[6]

However, for many other relationships we do keep monetized accounts. Nothing wrong with that. In large and complex societies, people need ample flows of money and a well-administered financial infrastructure in order to work together. For this purpose, money can be supplied like any other form of utility – like gas or electricity or internet bandwidth. Like these, it can be delivered by private enterprises but carefully regulated in the public interest.

But, as recent years have shown, governments have struggled to make financial institutions work in the public interest and in particular have been unable to control the creation and delivery of money. If the electricity grid operated in a similar fashion, bombarding our home with electricity one week and then deciding to cut many people off the next week, we would consider this intolerable. Heads would roll.

But finance seems different. Heads do not roll. Instead they insist on more comfortable pillows. Even in 2014, after a year of scandals and hefty fines for rigging markets, bankers, traders and city executives in London were still shrugging off all the criticism and treating themselves to bonuses averaging £125,000 ($200,000) each.[7] Those at the top did even better. A survey of 13 banks in London for 2014 showed that 2,600 employees were paid an average of £1.3 million ($2.1 million) each – around 50 times UK average annual pay.[8]

You would expect governments to step in. Unfortunately they seem unwilling. Instead they are somewhat in awe of the financial wizards and have been proud of applying a light regulatory touch. They have assumed that the financiers are sophisticated investors accustomed to taking risks and need little protection.

In reality, few people are capable of accurately assessing risk. Even the directors of investment funds have only the vaguest idea what their own staff are up to, and don't much care what the risks are, as long as this month's profit figures are good. As has become abundantly clear, however, while the high-rollers are willing to monopolize the rewards of success, they have been more 'generous' with the cost of their failures – forcing governments into rescue acts to stave off systemic collapses.

Perhaps, judged by their own criteria, the financial wizards are sophisticated. In fact, complexity is often a sign of incompetence. Any computer programmer knows that it takes only one slip in a line of code to generate unpredictable outcomes – and cause a computer to freeze. Similarly, some relatively straightforward operations on a ball of wool by the average cat will rapidly produce an almighty tangle of which Puss can be proud. The global financial system is similarly susceptible to incompetent management and regularly gets in a comparable mess.

How do we prevent this? First, we need to reconsider how money should be created. At present, licensed banks can conjure it up instantly. As explained in Chapter 2, if they see the potential for a loan to a reputable borrower who will pay good interest, they just create the money 'out of thin air' with a few taps on the keyboard.

This is very profitable for the banks – but for society it can be very costly. First, it exacerbates the tendency towards boom and bust. When the economy is growing, banks are happy to trust borrowers and create huge sums of money. Then, when millions of people are overextended, they try to cut their debts and the process swings into reverse. The supply of money suddenly contracts – and the whole economy along with it.

The booms and busts are often connected to property bubbles. As the US sub-prime crisis demonstrated only too clearly, financial markets awash with credit can land people with unmanageable debt – and lead to disaster. Easy credit can have longer-term implications. Soaring property prices have created a divide between those who were lucky enough to climb onto the property escalator early and those trying to do so now. This has driven a wedge between generations, making it impossible for many young people to buy homes. As indicated in the chart (on page 129), more than half of credit in the UK is for household mortgages – secured on dwellings. Back in 1997, in most areas of the UK, first-time buyers could buy a house with six years' average earnings; by 2014 this had stretched to 10 years' earnings.[9]

Leaving money creation in the hands of the banks not only encourages housing bubbles, it also narrows the government's scope for managing the economy. At present, if the government wishes to increase the money supply, it generally tries to do so by reducing interest rates. But reducing interest rates can also have the side-effect of encouraging reckless borrowing and lending.

When subsidizing banks, governments are also wasting a huge opportunity for 'seigniorage'. This refers to the income derived from issuing money. At present the potential for seigniorage is quite small. When the Bank of England, for example, prints new notes, it distributes them by selling them to commercial banks in exchange for payment in government bonds. These bonds pay 'interest' that can be passed to the Bank's sole shareholder, the Treasury.

However, this seigniorage is restricted, since the amount of additional banknotes issued each year is relatively small. Between November 2012 and October 2014, while the total money supply, created largely by the banks, rose by £1 billion, the value of notes and coins in circulation rose by only £6 million.[10] In 2014, the total money supply (termed M4) was £2.1 trillion but 97 per cent of this had been created by the banks as loans; only 3 per cent, £62 billion, had been issued as circulating notes and coins by the Bank of England. The Bank does issue around £10 billion in new notes each year, but also withdraws a lot as they wear out. In 2013, for instance, the British public claimed £12 million for damaged notes – torn, washed, chewed (that cat again), or otherwise mutilated.

The US government is in a similar situation, with the banks creating most of the money. At the end of 2014, the broadest measure of the US money supply (here M2) was $10.5 trillion, of which physical currency was $1.2 trillion – around 11 per cent.[11] This is a higher proportion of physical money than in the UK, partly because of differences in definition. But it is also because the paper US dollar is widely used abroad and many notes never return home. In some countries, such as Panama, this is because the government has dollarized the economy and the US dollar is used as a medium of exchange. In addition, people in many countries who distrust their own currency also hoard dollar bills as a store of wealth.

*The money crisis*

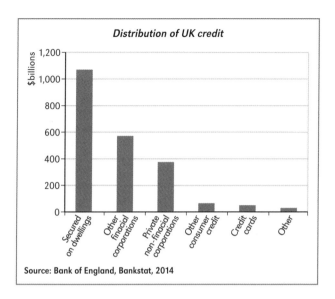

**Distribution of UK credit**

$billions

Source: Bank of England, Bankstat, 2014

As a result, more than half of US currency circulates abroad, mostly in the form of $100 bills.[12] Taking that into account, the proportion of physical money in the US is probably around five per cent.

The situation is similar in other countries. In Canada, for example, at the end of 2014, the total money supply (here M3) was C$1.9 trillion, of which around 3.7 per cent was currency.[13] In Australia the 'broad money' supply was A$1.7 trillion, of which 3.5 per cent was currency.[14]

Almost without knowing it, we have thus transferred huge and unaccountable power to the banks. In the UK, for example, a supposedly democratic country, most of the money supply is controlled by 56 unelected individuals – the directors of the major banks – HSBC (17), Barclays (14), RBS (11) Lloyds (13), and Standard Chartered (11). They create money with little heed to the needs of the national economy. Indeed, their interests often run counter to those of the rest of society. The more loans they make, the greater their profits, but this then increases the overhang of debt, with the corresponding levels of risk.

The major banks are huge and intricately entwined with national monetary systems, so any collapse has disastrous consequences. They have thus become 'too big to fail'. Any systemic bank that is about to go under is likely to be rescued by the government, even nationalized. This implied guarantee is very profitable for any bank since it makes the bank a much better credit risk. A bank that is underwritten by the government is unlikely to default and can borrow money more cheaply than it might otherwise have done. It can also take greater risks with that money. When these gambles pay off, the bank can garner large profits, pay its senior staff extravagantly and reward its shareholders. Should things go seriously wrong on all fronts, this will merely be inconvenient. The state will pick up the pieces. These implicit guarantees are hugely valuable to the banks. The IMF has estimated that in 2011-12 these subsidies were worth $15-$70 billion in the United States, $25-$110 billion in Japan, $20-$110 billion in the United Kingdom, and $90-$300 billion in the euro area.[15]

## Revoke licences to print money

What are the alternatives? There are two main approaches. One is to establish that only the state should be responsible for creating money – not just physical currency but all forms of money. Banks would no longer be able to create money out of thin air simply by adding new entries in their balance sheets. Instead they could only lend money that had been created by the government.

How would this work? It would primarily require making a sharp distinction between the money in your current account for transactions and the money in your savings account. In this new system, your current account would act as a sort of holding box and pay no interest. As now, you could use the money to pay bills, either in cash or electronically. But this money would not appear on the balance sheet of your bank. It would be money that belongs to you, just like banknotes in your wallet. At present, money in your bank account does not legally belong to you; the bank owes it to you as a debt.[16] You could carry out your usual transactions but you would pay a fee.

Banks would also offer loans, but they would do so in a much simpler fashion. Anything they lent would have to come from government-issued money deposited with them by savers, or borrowed from other banks, or from their tills, or from their own accounts held at the central bank. This is '100-per-cent reserve' banking. Instead of being backed by a small amounts of reserves at the central bank ('fractional reserve banking'), loans would need to derive entirely from government-issued money.

This would oblige banks to operate in a more transparent fashion and under greater public oversight. They would continue to offer services, for a suitable fee, and to make loans, but they would not be able to cream off extra profits by creating money. This is referred to as 'narrow banking'.

These ideas may seem radical and modern but they have a long pedigree. The principles were first articulated from the 1920s onwards by Frederick Soddy, a British Nobel prize winner for chemistry who turned his attention to economics.[17] The ideas were picked up in 1936 by, among others, US economist Irving Fisher.[18] This became known as the 'Chicago Plan', arguing that it would have a number of advantages – reducing large fluctuations in the business cycle, eliminating bank runs and dramatically reducing both public and private debt.

Just a few years ago, the idea still seemed unlikely to achieve any traction.[19] But it has steadily been taking hold. In 2010, for example, a former Governor of the Bank of England described the existing form of money creation as 'alchemy' and pointed out that a more fundamental reform would be to move away from fractional reserve banking.[20] Then, in 2012, researchers at the IMF concluded that Irving Fisher had been right on all counts.[21] The merits of 100-per-cent reserve banking have even surfaced in the pages of the *Financial Times*, whose chief economics editor in 2014 identified bank money creation as a 'giant hole at the heart of our market economies' and argued that this was rightly a function of the state.[22] Another notable development in the UK was the founding, in 2010, of the

### Sovereign money

Various mechanisms have been proposed for the introduction of sovereign money.[25] Some of the most detailed have come from the UK organization Positive Money.[26] They propose that the amount of new money to be created would be determined by a body independent of the government. This would estimate how much new money was needed to lubricate normal business at low levels of inflation. The body needs to be independent since governments would be tempted to pump in new money so as to make everyone feel richer prior to elections. The UK, for example, already has a Monetary Policy Committee which attempts to influence the supply indirectly by setting interest rates. The Central Bank would then create the money electronically and give it to the government.

This extra money could be injected into the economy in various ways. The first would be to finance additional government spending – by paying nurses more, for example. Or it could keep spending the same amount but cut taxes. Or it could pay off some of the national debt by buying back government bonds. Or, in an electronic form of 'helicopter money' it could simply make direct payments into the account of every citizen for them to spend as they like.

The banks would not be creating money but they would still have plenty to do. First, they would continue to manage payments and other transactions – debit cards, check books and non-profit organization Positive Money.[23] Now with sister organizations in 17 countries, this has been campaigning for the power to create money to be used in the public interest[24] (see box).

Under this proposal, an independent committee of monetary experts would estimate how much money the economy needs and authorize the central bank to create it. Rather than selling it to the banks, the government could then spend this money directly into the economy. This offers vastly greater seigniorage. Indeed, at normal rates of money creation, this might allow a government to fund the equivalent of a four-per-cent budget deficit without adding to the national debt.

This proposal has attracted supporters and opponents across the political spectrum. Critics argue that, if the

---

ATMs. However, for this purpose they would use only the money that originates in the central bank. The nurse's extra pay, for example, as well as his or her other money, would correspond to an entry in the records of the central bank. The bank cannot lend this out. So if the bank goes bust, the customer's funds still exist.

The second main bank function would be to do what most people think they do now – act as intermediaries between savers and borrowers. However, the mechanism would be different and more direct. Under this new scenario, the saver would transfer central-bank-created funds from their transaction account to a bank-administered pooled investment fund, rather like a unit trust. The bank would lend these funds as appropriate. Importantly, lending these funds would not create new money. As the fund paid out the loan, its account would shrink while that of the borrower would increase. However, as with any investment, the money would be at risk, and would not be underwritten by the government.

This would be a huge change – but it could take place gradually. The central bank would start to create money directly, in parallel with that created by banks. But over time the government could start to rein in bank lending by applying stricter regulations. This hybrid would continue until a determined date, after which all new money would be created by the government.

---

only money available is created by the government, this might seriously restrict the amount of money available. Better to retain the fairly elastic creation of money while regulating it more effectively.[27] And there are also concerns about putting so much power into the hands of an unelected committee. Nevertheless, one of the most important debates in monetary reform in the next few years will be on whether and how to implement sovereign money.

## Regulate the banks more effectively

Even if the sovereign money proposal were to be implemented in the long term, in the meantime it will still be important to regulate banks more effectively. These are some of the most important immediate issues.

### *Separate the banks from the casinos*

Universal banks carry out both basic banking and investment banking. Supposedly one acts as a buffer for the other. In practice, underlying government subsidies underwrite gambling. There are proposals to separate these functions. In the US, for example, banks are banned from using depositors' money to play the markets. In the UK and Europe, a current proposal is to try to 'ring-fence' customers' deposits from other activities. In the end both controls are likely to be leaky, open to interpretation and vulnerable to loopholes.

There are a number of stronger alternatives. One is to make a clear distinction between retail and investment banks and only allow government guarantees for retail banks. Another option is to establish a national payments infrastructure that the retail banks could use under licence. This would be analogous to train companies in the UK using infrastructure provided by Network Rail.[28] If one bank failed, this would not pose a systemic risk and its functions would be taken over by another company or temporarily by the state.

### Create greater diversity

A national payments system could also be accompanied by the establishment of a national bank to offer depositors and borrowers a different option – with stronger guarantees but less income from savings. But bank customers should have the overall choice as to which institutions to use –a state-owned bank offering the greatest security, a reasonably sized and well-run commercial bank, or a credit union, or, more likely, a mixture of two or more.

### Tax the transactions

Distortions and bubbles of all kinds are encouraged by electronic trading, which can see shares or currencies or bonds changing hands continuously at lightning speed. This encourages 'momentum' trading, which has nothing to do with underlying values and more to do with what other traders will do in the subsequent seconds or minutes. One of the most promising ways of addressing this, but as yet untried 40 years after it was proposed by Nobel laureate James Tobin, would be to tax every transaction. At present only around five per cent of currency trades, around $3 trillion per day, are linked to actual trade. The rest is speculation, which can wreak havoc with national budgets, especially for developing countries.

Applying a sales tax of around 0.2 per cent on each trade would skim off much of the speculative froth – while also generating valuable revenue. Assuming the annual trade were cut to a more reasonable level of $100 trillion, this would yield tax revenues of $200 billion for public purses. The same principle could be applied to stock exchanges, which would have the merit of stifling some of the endless churning of stocks in hedge funds, which achieves little other than the enrichment of traders and brokers.

### Close tax havens

The world's tax havens serve no purpose other than to boost the profits of corporations and rich individuals at the expense of regular taxpayers. The British government bears much of the responsibility, since it is in a position to exert direct control over some of its own territories. But there are other measures that could be taken to lift the veil of secrecy under which many companies and individuals operate, as they shuffle money from one dubious jurisdiction to another. This would involve, for example, demanding that companies declare the profits, losses and taxes they pay in every country in which they do business. Just as important would be to end banking secrecy and ensure that tax authorities in each country are able to exchange the necessary information.

## A fresh start

The global financial crisis had huge costs, not just for taxpayers in the rich countries but also for millions of people in developing countries who suffered the knock-on effects of global economic downturn. But this crisis should also be seen as an opportunity – to look again at the most basic assumptions about how money is created and used. Time for a fresh start.

**1** Oliver Bush, Samuel Knott and Chris Peacock, *Why is the UK banking system so big and is that a problem?* Topical articles, Bank of England, London, 2014. **2** Yalman Onaran, U.S. 'Banks Bigger Than GDP as Accounting Rift Masks Risk', Bloomberg.com, 23 February 2013. **3** Stewart Lansley and Howard Reed, *How to boost the wages share*, TUC Touchstone Pamphlets, London, 2012. **4** *Cost of a child: from cradle to college*, LV, 2014, nin.tl/costofachild **5** *Expenditures on Children by Families*, US Department of Agriculture, Washington, 2013. **6** *The bank of mum, not dad favoured by grown-up children*, nin.tl/bankofmumnotdad **7** Josephine Cumbo, 'Senior City workers expect bonuses to rise by a fifth', *Financial Times*, 22 December 2014. **8** 'RPT-Goldman tops UK banker pay with $4.7 million awarded for 2013', Reuters, 2015, nin.tl/topbankerpay2013 accessed 1 January. **9** Chris

Cross, 'The house prices-to-salaries map which shows why you may never get a mortgage', *Guardian*, 23 May 2014, nin.tl/housepricespiral **10** Bank of England, 2014, nin.tl/aboutbanknotes **11** US Federal Reserve, *Money Stock Measures – H.6,* 2014, nin.tl/Fedreserve accessed 31 December. **12** Ruth Judson, *Crisis and Calm: Demand for U.S. Currency at Home and Abroad from the Fall of the Berlin Wall to 2011*, International Finance Discussion Papers, no 1058, Board of Governors of the Federal Reserve System, Washington, 2012. **13** *Banking and Financial Statistics*, Bank of Canada, 2015 bankofcanada.ca/publications/bfs/ **14** *Statistical Tables,* Reserve Bank of Australia, 2015, nin.tl/Ausreserve **15** *IMF Financial Stability Report 2014*, IMF, Washington, 2014. **16** Toby Baxendale, 'What is the Legal Relationship Between the Banker and his Customer?' Cobden Centre, 2010, nin.tl/cobdencentre accessed 30 December 2014. **17** Frederick Soddy, *The role of money: What it should be contrasted with what it has become*. George Routledge and Sons, London, 1934. **18** Irving Fisher, '100% Money and the Public Debt', *Economic Forum*, April-June 1936, pp. 406-420. Available from thainsunset.com **19** J Huber & J Robertson, *Creating new money: A monetary reform for the information age,* New Economics Foundation, London, 2000. **20** Mervyn King, 'Banking: From Bagehot to Basel, and Back Again', The Second Bagehot Lecture, Buttonwood Gathering, New York City, 2010. **21** Jaromir Benes and Michael Kumhof, *The Chicago Plan Revisited*, IMF Working Paper 12/202, IMF, Washington, 2012. **22** Martin Wolf, 'Strip private banks of their power to create money', *Financial Times*, 14 August 2014. **23** positivemoney.org **24** Ben Dyson, Andrew Jackson, Graham Hodgson, *Creating a sovereign monetary system*, Positive Money, London,. 2014. **25** Steve Baker, 'Bank reform demands monetary reform', in *Banking 2020: A vision for the future,* ed Steve Tolley, New Economics Foundation, London, 2013. **26** Andrew Jackson and Ben Dyson, *Modernizing Money: Why our monetary system is broken, and how it can be fixed*, Positive Money, London, 2012. **27** Ann Pettifor, *Why I disagree with Martin Wolf and Positive Money*, 2014, nin.tl/annpettifor **28** Richard Murphy, 'Money banks and credit: A dilemma in search of an answer', Tax Research UK, 2014, nin.tl/taxresearchblog

# Index

Page numbers in **bold** refer to main subjects of boxed text.